Forge Your FUTURE

James Allen (1864–1912) retired from the business world to pursue a lifestyle of writing and contemplation. His books are classics in the fields of inspiration and spirituality. Although *As a Man Thinketh* is his most popular work, he authored several other books that deal with the power of thought, including *The Path of Prosperity, Eight Pillars of Prosperity* and *James Allen's Book of Meditations for Every Day in the Year.*

Forge Your FUTURE

Blueprint to Shape Your Life

JAMES ALLEN

RUPA

Published by
Rupa Publications India Pvt. Ltd 2024
7/16, Ansari Road, Daryaganj
New Delhi 110002

Sales centres:
Bengaluru Chennai
Hyderabad Jaipur Kathmandu
Kolkata Mumbai Prayagraj

P-ISBN: 978-93-5702-955-1
E-ISBN: 978-93-5702-901-8

First impression 2024

10 9 8 7 6 5 4 3 2 1

Printed in India

CONTENTS

1

MAN THE MASTER

By the mastery of self, a distinct form of consciousness is evolved which some would call divine. It is distinguished from that ordinary human consciousness, which craves personal advantages and gratifications on the one hand, and is involved in remorse and sorrow on the other. This divine consciousness concerns itself with humanity and the universe, with eternal verities, with righteousness, wisdom, and truth, and not with pleasures, protection, and preservation of the personality. Not that personal pleasure is destroyed, but that it is no longer craved and sought, it no longer takes a foremost place. It is purified, and it is received as the effect of right thought and action, and is no longer an end in itself.

In divine consciousness there is neither sin nor sorrow. Even the sense of sin has passed away, and the true order and purpose of life being revealed, no cause is found for lamentation. Jesus called this state of consciousness "The Kingdom of Heaven"; Buddha named it "Nirvana"; Lao-Tze's term for it was "Tao"; Emerson refers to it as "The Over-Soul"; and Dr. Bucke calls it "Cosmic Consciousness" in his valuable work bearing that title.

The ordinary human consciousness is self-consciousness. Self, the personality, is placed before everything else. There are ceaseless anxieties and fears concerning the self. Its possible loss is thought to be the most grievous calamity, and its eternal preservation the most important thing in the universe.

In divine consciousness all this has passed away. Self has disappeared. Therefore, there can be no more fears and anxieties concerning the self, and things are considered and known as they are, and not as they afford pleasure or cause pain to self, not as self wishes them to be for its own temporal or eternal happiness.

The self-conscious man is subject to desire; the divinely conscious man is master of desire. The former considers what is pleasant or unpleasant; the latter acts from the righteous law without reference to pleasure or pain.

The race is passing through self-consciousness to divine consciousness; through the slavery of self, with its sense of sin and shame, to the freedom of Truth, with its sense of purity and power. The Great Teachers and Saviors of the race have already attained. In former existences they have already passed through all forms of selfconsciousness, and now, having subjugated self, have become divinely conscious.

They have reached the summit of evolution on this earth, and have no further need to be reborn in the self-conscious form. They are Masters of Life. Having conquered self, they have acquired the Supreme Knowledge. Some of them are worshiped as God because they manifest a wisdom and a consciousness which is quite distinct from the normal self-consciousness of humanity, and which is therefore regarded with, and surrounded by, incomprehensible mystery. Yet, in this divine consciousness there is no mystery, but, on the contrary, a transparent simplicity which becomes apparent when the confusions of self are dispersed.

The abiding gentleness, the sublime wisdom, the perfect calm of the Great Teachers—qualities which appear supernatural when viewed from the selfconsciousness state—are seen to be simple and natural when the first glimmering of divine consciousness dawns in the mind. And such divine consciousness does not appear until a high degree of morality is attained by self-conscious man.

Man becomes divinely conscious, divinely wise, divinely gentle and strong in the measure that he subdues and dominates within, those passions by which humanity is subdued and dominated. The divine master is one who has attained mastery over self. The abiding nobility, beneficent characteristics, and unobtrusive virtue which mark off the spiritually enlightened man from others, are the fruits of self-conquest, the logical outcome of a long struggle to master and comprehend those mental forces which the self-conscious man blindly obeys without understanding.

ETERNAL CONQUERER

Self-conscious man is a slave to self. Obeying self-centered inclinations, he is in submission to his passions, and to the sorrows and pains which allegiance to those passions inflict upon him. He is conscious of sin and sorrow, but sees no way out of these conditions. And so he invents theologies which he substitutes for effort, and which, while affording him fitful comfort through uncertain hope, leave him the easy victim of sin, and the willing prey of sorrow.

Divinely conscious man is the master of self. He obeys Truth and not self. He curbs and directs his inclinations and is conscious of a growing power over sin and sorrow. He sees that there is a way out of these conditions by the path of self-mastery. He needs no theologies to aid him, but exerts himself in right-doing, and is gladdened by a sense of victory and increasing purity and power. When his mastery is complete, he has no inclinations but those which accord with Truth. He has then become the conqueror of sin, and is no longer subject to sorrow.

Enlightened, wise, and evermore peaceful and happy is he who has subjected, overcome, and cast out the turbulent self that reigned within. The tempests of sorrow do not chill him. The cares and troubles which beset man pass him by, and no evil thing overtakes him. Secure in divine virtue, no enemy can overthrow him; no foe can do harm. Kind and peaceful, no person, power, nor place can rob him of repose.

There is no enemy but self, no darkness but ignorance, no suffering but that which springs from the insubordinate elements of one's own nature.

No man is truly wise who is involved in likes and dislikes, wishes and regrets, desires and disappointments, sins and sorrow. All these conditions belong to the selfconscious state, and are indications of folly, weakness, and subjection.

He is truly wise who, in the midst of worldly duties, is always calm, always gentle, always patient. He accepts things as they are, and does not wish nor grieve, desire nor regret. These things belong to the divinely conscious state, the dominion of Truth, and are indications of enlightenment, strength, and mastery.

He who does not desire riches, fame, or pleasures; who enjoys what he has, yet does not lament when it is taken from him, he is indeed wise.

He who desires riches, fame, and pleasure; who is discontented with what he has, yet laments when it is taken from him, he is indeed foolish.

Man is fitted for conquest, but the conquest of territory will not avail; he must resort to the conquest of self. The conquest of territory renders man a temporal ruler, but the conquest of self makes him an eternal conqueror.

Man is destined for mastery; not the mastery of his fellow men by force, but the mastery of his own nature by self-control. The mastery of his fellow men by force is the crown of egotism, but the mastery of self by self-control is the crown of humility.

He is man the master who has shaken off the service of self for the service of Truth, who has established himself in the Eternal Verities. He is crowned, not only with perfect manhood, but with divine wisdom. He has overcome the disturbances of the mind and the shocks of life. He is superior to all circumstances. He is the calm spectator, but no longer the helpless tool, of events. No more a sinning, weeping, repenting mortal, he is pure, rejoicing, upright immortal. He perceives the course of things with a glad and peaceful heart; a divine conqueror, master of life and death.

2

MIND BUILDING AND LIFE BUILDING

Everything, both in nature and the works of man, is produced by a process of building. The rock is built up of atoms; the plant, the animal, and man are built up of cells; a house is built of bricks, and a book is built of letters. A world is composed of a large number of forms, and a city of a large number of houses. The arts, sciences, and institutions of a nation are built up by the efforts of individuals. The history of a nation is the building of its deeds.

The process of building necessitates the alternate process of breaking down. Old forms that have served their purpose are broken up, and the material of which they are composed enters into new combinations. There is reciprocal integration and disintegration. In all compounded bodies, old cells are ceaselessly being broken up, and new cells are formed to take their place.

The works of man also require to be continually renewed until they have become old and useless, when they are torn down in order that some better purpose may be served. These two processes of breaking down and building up in Nature are called death and life; in the artificial works of man they are called destruction and restoration.

This dual process, which obtains universally in things visible, also obtains universally in things invisible. As a body is built of cells, and a house of bricks, so a man's mind is built of thoughts. The various characters of men are none other than compounds of thoughts of varying combinations. Herein we see the deep truth of the saying, "As a man thinketh in his heart, so is he." Individual characteristics are fixed processes of thought; that is, they are fixed in the sense that they have become such an integral part of the character that they can be only altered or removed by a protracted effort of the will, and by much self-discipline. Character is built in the same way as a tree or a house is built—namely, by the ceaseless addition of new material, and that material is thought. By the aid of millions of bricks a city is built; by the aid of millions of thoughts a mind, a character, is built.

Every man is a mind builder, whether he recognizes it or not. Every man must perforce think, and every thought is another brick laid down in the edifice of mind. Such "brick laying" is done loosely and carelessly by a vast number of people, the result being unstable and tottering characters that are ready to go down under the first little gust of trouble or temptation.

Some, also, put into the building of their minds large numbers of impure thoughts; these are so many rotten bricks that crumble away as fast as they are put in, leaving always an unfinished and unsightly building, and one which can afford no comfort and no shelter for its possessor.

Debilitating thoughts about one's health, enervating thoughts concerning unlawful pleasures, weakening thoughts of failure, and sickly thoughts of self-pity and self-praise are useless bricks with which no substantial mind temple can be raised.

Pure thoughts, wisely chosen and well placed, are so many durable bricks which will never crumble away, and from which a finished and beautiful building, and one which affords comfort and shelter for its possessor, can be rapidly erected.

Bracing thoughts of strength, of confidence, of duty; inspiring thoughts of a large, free, unfettered, and unselfish life, are useful bricks with which a substantial mind temple can be raised; and the building of such a temple necessitates that old and useless habits of thought be broken down and destroyed.

"Build thee more stately mansions, O my soul! As the swift seasons roll."

Each man is the builder of himself. If he is the occupant of a jerry-built hovel of a mind that lets in the rains of many troubles, and through which blow the keen winds of oft-recurring disappointments, let him get to work to build a more noble mansion which will afford him better protection against those mental elements. Trying to weakly shift the responsibility for his jerry-building on to the devil, or his forefathers, or anything or anybody but himself, will neither add to his comfort, nor help him to build a better habitation.

When he wakes up to a sense of his responsibility, and an approximate estimate of his power, then he will commence to build like a true workman, and will produce a symmetrical and finished character that will endure, and be cherished by posterity, and which, while affording a never failing protection for himself, will continue to give shelter to many a struggling one when he has passed away.

The whole visible universe is framed on a few mathematical principles. All the wonderful works of man in the material world have been brought about by the rigid observance of a few underlying principles; and all that there is to the making of a successful, happy, and beautiful life, is the knowledge and application of a few simple, root principles.

If a man is to erect a building that is to resist the fiercest storms, he must build it on a simple, mathematical principle, or law, such as the square or the circle; if he ignores this, his edifice will topple down even before it is finished.

Likewise, if a man is to build up a successful, strong, and exemplary life—a life that will stoutly resist the fiercest storms of adversity and temptation—it must be framed on a few simple, undeviating moral principles.

Four of these principles are Justice, Rectitude, Sincerity, and Kindness. These four ethical truths are to the making of a life what the four lines of a square are to the building of a house. If a man ignores them and thinks to obtain success and happiness and peace by injustice, trickery, and selfishness, he is in the position of a builder who imagines he can build a strong and durable habitation while ignoring the relative arrangement of mathematical lines, and he will, in the end, obtain only disappointment and failure.

He may, for a time, make money, which will delude him into believing that injustice and dishonesty pay well; but in reality his life is so weak and unstable that it is ready at any moment to fall; and when a critical period comes, as come it must, his affairs, his reputation, and his riches crumble to ruins, and he is buried in his own desolation.

It is totally impossible for a man to achieve a truly successful and happy life who ignores the four moral principles enumerated, whilst the man who scrupulously observes them in all his dealings can no more fail of success and blessedness than the earth can fail of the light and warmth of the sun so long as it keeps to its lawful orbit; for he is working in harmony with the fundamental laws of the universe; he is building his life on a basis which cannot be altered or overthrown, and, therefore, all that he does will be so strong and durable, and all the parts of his life will be so coherent, harmonious, and firmly knit that it cannot possibly be brought to ruin.

THE FOUNDATION OF HAPPINESS

In all the universal forms which are built up by the Great Invisible and unerring Power, it will be found that the observance of mathematical law is carried out with unfailing exactitude down to the most minute detail. The microscope reveals the fact that the infinitely small is as perfect as the infinitely great.

A snowflake is as perfect as a star. Likewise, in the erection of a building by man, the strictest attention must be paid to every detail.

A foundation must first be laid, and, although it is to be buried and hidden, it must receive the greatest care, and be made stronger than any other part of the building; then stone upon stone, brick upon brick is carefully laid with the aid of the plumb line, until at last the building stands complete in its durability, strength, and beauty.

Even so it is with the life of a man. He who would have a life secure and blessed, a life freed from the miseries and failures to which so many fall victims, must carry the practice of the moral principles into every detail of his life, into every momentary duty and trivial transaction. In every little thing he need be thorough and honest, neglecting nothing.

To neglect or misapply any little detail—be he commercial man, agriculturist, professional man, or artisan—is the same as neglecting a stone or a brick in a building, and it will be a source of weakness and trouble.

The majority of those who fail and come to grief do so through neglecting the apparently insignificant details.

It is a common error to suppose that little things can be passed by, and that the greater things are more important, and should receive all attention; but a cursory glance at the universe, as well as a little serious reflection on life, will teach the lesson that nothing great can exist which is not made up of small details, and in the composition of which every detail is perfect.

He who adopts the four ethical principles as the law and base of his life, who raises the edifice of character upon them, who in his thoughts and words and actions does not wander from them, whose every duty and every passing transaction is performed in strict accordance with their exactions, such a man, laying down the hidden foundation of integrity of heart securely and strongly, cannot fail to raise up a structure which shall bring him honor; and he is building a temple in which he can repose in peace and blessedness—even the strong and beautiful Temple of his life.

3

VISIONS AND IDEALS

The dreamers are the saviours of the world. As the visible world is sustained by the invisible, so men, through all their trials and sins and sordid vocations, are nourished by the beautiful visions of their solitary dreamers. Humanity cannot forget its dreamers; it cannot let their ideals fade and die; it lives in them; it knows them as they realities which it shall one day see and know.

Composer, sculptor, painter, poet, prophet, sage, these are the makers of the after-world, the architects of heaven. The world is beautiful because they have lived; without them, labouring humanity would perish.

He who cherishes a beautiful vision, a lofty ideal in his heart, will one day realize it. Columbus cherished a vision of another world, and he discovered it; Copernicus fostered the vision of a multiplicity of worlds and a wider universe, and he revealed it; Buddha beheld the vision of a spiritual world of stainless beauty and perfect peace, and he entered into it.

Cherish your visions; cherish your ideals; cherish the music that stirs in your heart, the beauty that forms in your mind, the loveliness that drapes your purest thoughts, for out of them will grow all delightful conditions, all, heavenly environment; of these, if you but remain true to them, your world will at last be built.

To desire is to obtain; to aspire is to, achieve. Shall man's basest desires receive the fullest measure of gratification, and his purest aspirations starve for lack of sustenance? Such is not the Law: such a condition of things can never obtain: "ask and receive."

Dream lofty dreams, and as you dream, so shall you become. Your Vision is the promise of what you shall one day be; your Ideal is the prophecy of what you shall at last unveil.

The greatest achievement was at first and for a time a dream. The oak sleeps in the acorn; the bird waits in the egg; and in the highest vision of the soul a waking angel stirs. Dreams are the seedlings of realities.

BECOMING YOUR VISION

Your circumstances may be uncongenial, but they shall not long remain so if you but perceive an Ideal and strive to reach it. You cannot travel within and stand still without. Here is a youth hard pressed by poverty and labour; confined long hours in an unhealthy workshop; unschooled, and lacking all the arts of refinement. But he dreams of better things; he thinks of intelligence, of refinement, of grace and beauty. He conceives of, mentally builds up, an ideal condition of life; the vision of a wider liberty and a larger scope takes possession of him; unrest urges him to action, and he utilizes all his spare time and means, small though they are, to the development of his latent powers and resources. Very soon so altered has his mind become that the workshop can no longer hold him. It has become so out of harmony with his mentality that it falls out of his life as a garment is cast aside, and, with the growth of opportunities, which fit the scope of his expanding powers, he passes out of it forever. Years later we see this youth as a full-grown man. We find him a master of certain forces of the mind, which he wields with worldwide influence and almost unequalled power. In his hands he holds the cords of gigantic responsibilities; he speaks, and lo, lives are changed; men and women hang upon his words and remould their characters, and, sunlike, he becomes the fixed and luminous centre round which innumerable destinies revolve. He has realized the Vision of his youth. He has become one with his Ideal.

And you, too, youthful reader, will realize the Vision (not the idle wish) of your heart, be it base or beautiful, or a mixture of both, for you will always gravitate toward that which you, secretly, most love. Into your hands will be placed the exact results of your own thoughts; you will receive that which you earn; no more, no less. Whatever your present environment may be, you will fall, remain, or rise with your thoughts, your Vision, your Ideal. You will become as small as your controlling desire; as great as your dominant aspiration: in the beautiful words of Stanton Kirkham Davis, "You may be keeping accounts, and presently you shall walk out of the door that for so long has seemed to you the barrier of your ideals, and shall find yourself before an audience—the pen still behind your ear, the ink stains on your fingers and then and there shall pour out the torrent of your inspiration. You may be driving sheep, and you shall wander to the city-bucolic and open-mouthed; shall wander under the intrepid guidance of the spirit into the studio of the master, and after a time he shall say, 'I have nothing more to teach you.' And now you have become the master, who did so recently dream of great things while driving sheep. You shall lay down the saw and the plane to take upon yourself the regeneration of the world."

The thoughtless, the ignorant, and the indolent, seeing only the apparent effects of things and not the things themselves, talk of luck, of fortune, and chance. Seeing a man grow rich, they say, "How lucky he is!" Observing another become intellectual, they exclaim, "How highly favoured he is!" And noting the saintly character and wide influence of another, they remark, "How chance aids him at every turn!" They do not see the trials and failures and struggles which these men have voluntarily encountered in order to gain their experience; have no knowledge of the sacrifices they have made, of the undaunted efforts they have put forth, of the faith they have exercised, that they might overcome the apparently insurmountable, and realize the Vision of their heart. They do not know the darkness and the heartaches; they only see the light and joy, and call it "luck". They do not see the long and arduous journey, but only behold the pleasant goal, and call it "good fortune," do not understand the process, but only perceive the result, and call it chance.

In all human affairs there are efforts, and there are results, and the strength of the effort is the measure of the result. Chance is not. Gifts, powers, material, intellectual, and spiritual possessions are the fruits of effort; they are thoughts completed, objects accomplished, visions realized.

The Vision that you glorify in your mind, the Ideal that you enthrone in your heart—this you will build your life by, this you will become.

4

FAITH AND COURAGE

For those who will fight bravely and not yield, there is triumphant victory over all the dark things of life. I state this at the beginning, that the reader may know there is no uncertainty about it. In the course of this book I shall show what are the elements, in character and conduct, which go to build up the life of calm strength and superlative victory.

To stand face to face with truth; to arrive, after innumerable wanderings and pains, at wisdom and bliss; not to be finally defeated and cast out, but ultimately to triumph over every inward foe—such is man's divine destiny, such his glorious goal. And this, every saint, sage, and savior has declared.

In the present stage of the life of humanity, comparatively few reach this place of triumph—though all will reach it at last—yet there is a glorious company of perfect ones who have attained in the past, and their number is being added to with each succeeding age. Men are as yet learners in the school of life, and most men die learners. But there are some who, in this life, through fixity of purpose and strenuous fighting against darkness, pain, and ignorance, acquire a right knowledge of life and pass joyfully beyond the pupil stage.

Man is not to remain forever a schoolboy in the universe, to be whipped for follies and errors. When he wills and wishes, he can set his mind upon his task and master the lessons of life, becoming a confident and skilled scholar, living in understanding and peace, and not in ignorance and misery.

The sorrows of life are profound and deeply rooted, but they can be fathomed and rooted out. The passions and emotions of human nature are, in their ungoverned state, overwhelming and painfully conflicting, but they can be so softened down, harmonized, and wisely directed and understood, as to become obedient servants for the outworking of enlightened purposes.

The difficulties of life are great, its battle fierce, and its wished-for issues are uncertain and elusive; so much so, that every hour men and women are breaking down under the strain. Yet these conditions have no objective and arbitrary existence. In their true nature they are subjective and purely mental, and can be transcended. There is no inherent and permanent evil in the universal order; and the mind can be lifted up to the moral altitude where evil can touch it no more.

A steadfast faith in an Eternal and Universal Justice, in an over-ruling Good, is the prelude to the Life Triumphant. The man who aims to become strong, serene, and steadfast at heart must, at the onset, have no doubt that the Heart of Life is good. He who is to gaze upon the Cosmic Order and experience the rapture of emancipation must realize that there is no disorder in his life but that which he creates. This realization is difficult, so prone is the mind, in its imperfect stages, to self-pity and self-justification, but it can be attained, and must be attained by him who is to live the freed life. At first it must be believed, and the belief must be adhered to, until it ripens into realization and knowledge.

The sufferings of life are greatly reduced when they are accepted as disciplinary experiences, and the man of faith does so accept them. The sufferings of life are transcended and put away when all experiences are accounted good, and are utilized in the development of character, and the man of knowledge does so regard and utilize them.

BELIEVE IN THE COSMIC FORCE

Faith is the grey dawn which precedes the full and perfect day of knowledge. Without it there can be no attainment of strength, no permanent security of heart. The man of faith does not succumb when difficulties present themselves; he does not despair when troubles overtake him. However steep and dark his path may seem, he looks forward to a brighter pathway ahead. He sees a destination of rest and light beyond. They who have no faith in the triumph of good ignominiously succumb to the elements of evil. And this must be so; for he who does not elevate good, elevates evil, and, seeing evil as the master of life, he receives the wages of evil.

There are those who, having yielded to defeat in the battle of life, talk thoughtlessly about the wrongs they have suffered at the hands of others. They believe—and try to make others believe—that they would have been successful or rich or famous but for the treachery and villainy of those about them. They tell, for the thousandth time, how they have been deceived, defrauded, and degraded by others. They imagine that they themselves are all trust, all innocence, all honesty and good nature, and that nearly everyone else is all that is bad and malicious. They tell how they would have been just as prosperous and honored as others if they had been as selfish as those others; and that their great drawback, and the chief source, in themselves, of their failures, is that they were born with too great an endowment of unselfishness.

Such self-praising complainers cannot distinguish between

good and evil, and their faith in human nature and the goodness of the universe is dead. Looking upon others, they have eyes for evil only; looking upon themselves, they see only suffering innocence. Rather than discover any evil in themselves, they would have all humanity bad. In their hearts they have enthroned the wretched Demon of Evil as the Lord of Life, and see in the course of things only a selfish scramble in which the good is always crushed and the evil rises triumphant. Blind to their own folly, ignorance, and weakness, they see nothing but injustice in their fate, nothing but misery and wretchedness in their present condition.

He who would have even a useful and successful life—yet alone a spiritually noble and victorious one—must at once root out and cast away this wretched condition of mind that negates all that is good and pure, and gives preeminence to all that is base and impure. Misfortune, misery and defeat most surely await the man who believes that dishonesty, deceit and selfishness are the best weapons whereby to achieve a successful life. What courage and strength can a man develop, and what quiet and happiness can he enjoy, who believes that in order to keep pace with others he must continually deny and discourage the better qualities of his nature? The man who believes that evil is more powerful than good, and that bad men have the best of life, is still involved in the elements of evil; and, being so involved, he suffers—must necessarily suffer—defeat.

It may appear to you that the world is given over to wickedness; that the bad prosper, and the good fail; that there is nothing but chance, injustice, and disorder. But do not believe this: regard it as an elusive appearance. Conclude that you do not see life as it really is; that you have not yet fathomed the causes of things, and that when you can look upon life through a purer heart and a wiser mind, you will see and understand its equity. And truly when you do so look at life, you will see good where you now see evil, order where now appears disorder, and justice where now injustice seems to prevail.

The universe is a cosmos, not a chaos, and the bad do not prosper. It is true there is much evil in the world, otherwise there would be no necessity for moral aims, but there is also much misery in the world, and the evil and misery are related as cause and effect. It is equally true that there is much good in the world, and much abiding gladness, and the good and gladness are related as cause and effect. He who has acquired that faith in the power and supremacy of good, which no apparent injustice, no amount of suffering, and no catastrophe can shake, will pass through all emergencies, all trials and difficulties, with a sublime courage that defies the demons of doubt and despair. He may not succeed in all his plans. He may even encounter much failure; but when he fails, it will be that he may frame nobler purposes and ascend to higher achievements. He will only fail in order to reach a success greater than that of which he first dreamed. His life will not, cannot, be a failure. Some of its details will fail, but this will be but the breaking of weak links in the chain of character and events, in order that the whole may be made more strong and complete.

There is an animal courage which can calmly face the fire of an enemy in battle, or the fierce rage of beasts, but which fails in the battle of life and breaks down when confronted with the beasts that rage within one's own heart. It requires a higher, diviner courage to remain calm in the hour of deprivation and calamity than in the heat of battle, to overcome self than to overcome another. And this diviner courage is the companion of faith.

A mere theological belief (commonly confused with faith)

will not avail. Beliefs about God, Jesus, Creation, etc., are merely surface opinions (derived chiefly from custom) which do not reach down to the real life of a man and have no power to bestow faith. Such beliefs may accompany faith, but they are distinct from it. Frequently, those who hold most tenaciously to particular beliefs about God, Jesus, and the Bible are most lacking in faith—that is, they give way to complaint, despondency, and grief immediately after some petty trouble overtakes them. If one is given to irritability, anxiety, hopelessness, and lamentations over the simple things of life, let him know that, in spite of his religious belief or metaphysical philosophy, he lacks faith. For where faith is there is courage, there is fortitude, there is steadfastness and strength.

The opinions of men are lightly to be considered, for they are changing with every new breeze of thought. They have very little part in the reality of things, being the bubbles of a surface effervescence. But behind all opinions there is the same human heart. The "godless" are they who are goodless, even though they may be members of churches and make a great profession of faith in God. The "godly" are they who are goodly even though they make no profession of religion. The complainers and bewailers are the faithless and unbelieving. Those who deny or belittle the power of good, and in their lives and actions affirm and magnify the power of evil, are the only real atheists.

Faith bestows that sublime courage that rises superior to the petty and selfish disappointments and troubles of life, that acknowledges no defeat except as a step to victory; that is strong to endure, patient to wait, and energetic to struggle. It perceives the benign law of Truth in all things, and is assured of the final triumph of the heart, and the kingly power of the mind.

Light up, then, the lamp of faith in your heart, and walk

through the darkness guided by its illuminating rays. Its light is dim, and cannot be compared with the sunlight brilliance of knowledge, but it suffices to lead one safely through the mists of doubt and the black darkness of despair; along the narrow, thorny ways of sickness and sorrow, and over the treacherous planes of temptation and uncertainty. It enables man to ward off and outstrip the foul beasts that rage in the jungle of his heart, and to reach safely the open plains of a pure life and the mountain levels of conquest where the dim light of faith is no longer needed. For, leaving behind him all the darkness, all the doubt, error, and sorrow, he enters into a new consciousness and upon a higher round of life, works, and acts, and lives self-contained and peaceful, in the full and glorious light of knowledge.

5

THOROUGHNESS

Thoroughness consists in doing little things as though they were the greatest things in the world. That the little things of life are of primary importance, is a truth not generally understood, and the thought that little things can be neglected, thrown aside, or slurred over, is at the root of that lack of thoroughness which is so common, and which results in imperfect work and unhappy lives.

When one understands that the great things of the world and of life consist of a combination of small things, and that without this aggregation of small things the great things would be nonexistent, then he begins to pay careful attention to those things which he formerly regarded as insignificant. He Thus, acquires the quality of thoroughness, and becomes a man of usefulness and influence; for the possession or non-possession of this one quality may mean all the difference between a life of peace and power, and one of misery and weakness.

Every employer of labor knows how comparatively rare this quality is—how difficult it is to find men and women who will put thought and energy into their work, and do it completely and satisfactorily. Bad workmanship abounds. Skill and excellence are acquired by few. Thoughtlessness, carelessness, and laziness are such common vices that it should cease to appear strange that, in spite of "social reform," the ranks of the unemployed should continue to swell, for those who scamp their work today will, another day, in the hour of deep necessity, look and ask for work in vain.

FORSAKE UNTIMELY PLEASURE

The law of the survival of the fittest is not based on cruelty, it is based on justice: it is one aspect of that divine equity which everywhere prevails. Vice is "beaten with many stripes"; if it were not so, how could virtue be developed? The thoughtless and lazy cannot take precedence of, or stand equally with, the thoughtful and industrious. A friend of mine tells me that his father gave all his children the following piece of advice:

"Whatever your future work may be, put your whole mind upon it and do it thoroughly; you need then have no fear as to your welfare, for there are so many who are careless and negligent that the services of the thorough man are always in demand."

I know those who have, for years, tried almost in vain to secure competent workmanship in spheres which do not require exceptional skill, but which call chiefly for forethought, energy, and conscientious care. They have discharged one after another for negligence, laziness, incompetence, and persistent breaches of duty—not to mention other vices which have no bearing on this subject; yet the vast army of the unemployed continues to cry out against the laws, against society, and against Heaven.

The cause of this common lack of thoroughness is not far to seek; it lies in that thirst for pleasure which not only creates a distaste for steady labor, but renders one incapable of doing the best work, and of properly fulfilling one's duty. A short time ago, a case came under my observation (one of many such), of a poor woman who was given, at her earnest appeal, a responsible and lucrative position. She had been at her post only a few days when she began to talk of the "pleasure trips" she was going to have now she had come to that place. She was discharged at the end of a month for negligence and incompetence.

As two objects cannot occupy the same space at the same time, so the mind that is occupied with pleasure cannot also be concentrated upon the perfect performance of duty.

Pleasure has its own place and time, but its consideration should not be allowed to enter the mind during those hours which should be devoted to duty. Those who, while engaged in their worldly task, are continually dwelling upon anticipated pleasures, cannot do otherwise than bungle through their work, or even neglect it when their pleasure seems to be at stake.

Thoroughness is completeness, perfection; it means doing a thing so well that there is nothing left to be desired; it means doing one's work, if not better than anyone else can do it, at least not worse than the best that others do. It means the exercise of much thought, the putting forth of great energy, the persistent application of the mind to its task, the cultivation of patience, perseverance, and a high sense of duty. An ancient teacher said, "If anything has to be done, let a man do it, let him attack it vigorously"; and another teacher said, "Whatsoever thy hand findeth to do, do it with thy might."

He who lacks thoroughness in his worldly duties, will also lack the same quality in spiritual things. He will not improve his character; will be weak and half-hearted in his religion, and will not accomplish any good and useful end. The man who keeps one eye on worldly pleasure and the other on religion, and who thinks he can have the advantage of both conditions, will not be thorough either in his pleasure seeking or his religion, but will make a sorry business of both. It is better to be a whole-souled worldling than a half-hearted religionist; better to give the entire mind to a lower thing than half of it to a higher.

It is preferable to be thorough, even if it be in a bad or selfish direction, rather than inefficient and squeamish in good directions, for thoroughness leads more rapidly to the development of character and the acquisition of wisdom; it accelerates progress and unfoldment; and while it leads the bad to something better, it spurs the good to higher and ever higher heights of usefulness and power.

6

THE MIGHT OF MEEKNESS

The mountain bends not to the fiercest storm, but it shields the fledgling and the lamb; and though all men tread upon it, yet it protects them, and bears them up upon its deathless bosom. Even so is it with the meek man who, though shaken and disturbed by none, yet compassionately bends to shield the lowliest creature, and, though he may be despised, lifts all men up. and lovingly protects them.

As glorious as the mountain in its silent is the divine man in his silent Meekness; like its form, his loving comparison is expansive and sublime. Truly his body, like the mountain's base, is fixed in the valleys and the mists; but the summit of his being is eternally bathed in cloudless glory, and lives with the Silences.

He who has found Meekness has found divinity; he has realized the divine consciousness, and knows himself as divine. He also knows all others as divine, though they know it not themselves, being asleep and dreaming. Meekness is a divine quality, and as such is all powerful. The meek man overcomes by not resisting, and by allowing himself to be defeated he attains to the Supreme Conquest.

The man who conquers another by force is strong; the man who conquers himself by Meekness is mighty. He who conquers another by force will himself likewise be conquered; he who conquers himself by Meekness will never be overthrown, for the human cannot overcome the divine. The meek man is triumphant in defeat. Socrates lives the more by being put to death; in the crucified Jesus the risen Christ is revealed, and Stephen in receiving his stoning defies the hurting power of stones. That which is real cannot be destroyed, but only that which is unreal. When a man finds that within him which is real, which is constant, abiding, changeless, and eternal, he enters into that Reality, and becomes meek. All the powers of darkness will come against him. but they will do him no hurt, and will at last, depart from him.

MEEKNESS: A WAY OF LIFE

The meek man is found in the time of trial; when other men fall he stands. His patience is not destroyed by the foolish passions of others, and when they come against him he does not "strive nor cry," He knows the utter powerlessness of all evil, having overcome it in himself, and lives in the changeless strength and power of divine Good.

Meekness is one aspect of the operation of that changeless Love which is at the Heart of all things, and is therefore an imperishable quality. He who lives in it is without fear, knowing the Highest, and having the lowest under his feet.

The meek man shines in darkness, and flourishes in obscurity. Meekness cannot boast, nor advertise itself, nor thrive on popularity. It is practised, and is seen or not seen; being a spiritual quality it is perceived only by the eye of the spirit. Those who are not spiritually awakened see it not, nor do they love it, being enamoured of, and blinded by, worldly shows and appearances. Nor does history take note of the meek man. Its glory is that of strife and self-aggrandizement; his is the glory of peace and gentleness. History chronicles the earthly, not the heavenly acts. Yet though he lives in obscurity he cannot be hidden (how can light be hid?); he continues to shine after he has withdrawn himself from the world, and is worshipped by the world which knew him not.

That the meek man should be neglected, abused, or misunderstood is reckoned by him as of no account, and therefore not to be considered, much less resisted. He knows that all such weapons are the flimsiest and most ineffectual of shadows. To them, therefore, who give him evil he gives good. He resists none, and thereby conquers all.

He who imagines he can be injured by others, and who seeks to justify and defend himself against them, does not understand Meekness, does not comprehend the essence and meaning of life. "He abused me, he beat me, he defeated me, he robbed me.—In those who harbour such thoughts hatred will never cease . . . for hatred ceases not by hatred at any time; hatred ceases by love." What sayest thou, thy neighbour has spoken thee falsely? Well, what of that? Can a falsity hurt thee? That which is false is false, and there is an end of it. It is without life, and without power to hurt any but him who seeks to hurt by it. It is nothing to thee that thy neighbour should speak falsely of thee, but it is much to thee that thou shouldst resist him, and seek to justify thyself, for, by so doing, thou givest life and vitality to thy neighbour's falseness, so that thou art injured and distressed. Take all evil out of thine own heart, then shalt thou see the folly of resisting it in another. Thou wilt be trodden on? Thou art trodden on already if thou thinkest thus. The injury that thou seest as coming from another comes only from thyself. The wrong thought, or word, or act of another has no power to hurt thee unless thou galvanize it into life by thy passionate resistance, and so receivest it into thyself. If any man slander me, that is his concern, not mine. I have to do with my own soul, not with my neighbour's. Though all the world misjudge me, it is no business of mine; but that I should possess my soul in Purity and Love, that is all my business. There shall be no end to strife until men cease to justify themselves. He who would have wars cease let him cease to defend any party—let him cease to defend himself. Not by strife can peace come, but by ceasing from strife. The glory of Cæsar resides in the resistance of his enemies. They resist and fall. Give to Cæsar that which Cæsar demands, and Cæsar's glory and power are gone. Thus, by submission does the meek man conquer the strong man : but it is not that outward show of submission which is slavery, it is that inward and spiritual submission which is freedom.

Claiming no rights, the meek man is not troubled with self-defence and self-justification; he lives in love, and therefore comes under the immediate and vital protection of the Great Love which is the Eternal Law of the universe. He neither claims nor seeks his own; Thus, do all things come to him, and all the universe shields and protects him.

He who says, "I have tried Meekness, and it has failed," has not tried Meekness. It cannot be tried as an experiment. It is only arrived at by unreserved self-sacrifice. Meekness does not consist merely in non-resistance in action; it consists pre-eminently in non-resistance in thought, in ceasing to hold or to have any selfish, condemnatory, or retaliatory thoughts. The meek man, therefore, cannot "take offence" or have his "feelings hurt," living above hatred, folly, and vanity. Meekness can never fail.

O thou who searchest for the Heavenly Life! strive after Meekness; increase thy patience and forbearance day by day; bid thy tongue cease from all harsh words; withdraw thy mind from selfish arguments, and refuse to brood upon thy wrongs: so living, thou shalt carefully tend and cultivate the pure and delicate flower of Meekness in thy heart, until at last, its divine sweetness and purity and beauteous perfection shall be revealed to thee, and thou shalt become gentle, joyful, and strong. Repine not that thou art surrounded by irritable and selfish people; but rather rejoice that thou art so favoured as to have thine own imperfections revealed to thee, and that thou art so placed as to necessitate within thee a constant struggle for self-mastery and the attainment, of perfection. The more there is of harshness and selfishness around thee the greater is the need of thy Meekness and love. If others seek to wrong thee, all the more is it needful that thou shouldst cease from all wrong, and live in love; if others preach Meekness, humility, and love, and do not practice these, trouble not nor be annoyed; but do thou, in the silence of thy heart, and in thy contact with others, practice these things, and they shall preach themselves. And though thou utter no declamatory word, and stand before no gathered audience, thou shalt teach the whole world. As thou becomest meek, thou shalt learn the deepest secrets of the universe. Nothing is hidden from him who overcomes himself. Into the cause of causes shalt thou penetrate, and lifting, one after another, every veil of illusion, shalt reach at last the inmost Heart of Being. Thus, becoming one with Life, thou shalt know till life, and, seeing into causes, and knowing realities, thou shalt be no more anxious about thyself, and others, and the world, but shalt see that all things that are, are engines of the Great Law. Canopied with gentleness, thou shalt bless where others curse; love where others hate; forgive where others condemn; yield where others strive; give up where others grasp: lose where others gain, And in their strength they shall be weak; and in thy weakness thou shalt be strong; yea, thou shalt mightily prevail. He that hath not unbroken gentleness hath not Truth:

"Therefore when Heaven would save a man, it enfolds him with gentleness."

7

YOUR MENTAL ATTITUDE

As a being of thought, your dominant mental attitude will determine your condition in life. It will also be the gauge of your knowledge and the measures of your attainment. The so-called limitations of your nature are the boundary lines of your thoughts; they are self-erected fences, and can be drawn to a narrower circle, extended to a wider, or be allowed to remain.

You are the thinker of your thoughts and as such you are the maker of yourself and condition. Thought is causal and creative, and appears in your character and life in the form of results. There are no accidents in your life. Both its harmonies and antagonisms are the responsive echoes of your thoughts. A man thinks, and his life appears.

If your dominant mental attitude is peaceable and lovable, bliss and blessedness will follow you; if it be resistant and hateful, trouble and distress will cloud your pathway. Out of ill-will will come grief and disaster; out of good-will, healing and reparation.

You imagine your circumstances as being separate from yourself, but they are intimately related to your thought world. Nothing appears without an adequate cause. Everything that happens is just. Nothing is fated, everything is formed.

As you think, you travel; as you love, you attract. You are today where your thoughts have brought you; you will be tomorrow where your thoughts take you. You cannot escape the result of your thoughts, but you can endure and learn, can accept and be glad.

You will always come to the place where your love (your most abiding and intense thought) can receive its measure of gratification. If your love be base, you will come to a base place; if it be beautiful, you will come to a beautiful place. You can alter your thoughts, and so alter your condition. Strive to perceive the vastness and grandeur of your responsibility. You are powerful, not powerless. You are as powerful to obey as you are to disobey; as strong to be pure as to be impure; as ready for wisdom as for ignorance. You can learn what you will, can remain as ignorant as you choose. If you love knowledge you will obtain it; if you love wisdom you will secure it; if you love purity you will realise it. All things await your acceptance, and you choose by the thoughts which you entertain.

A man remains ignorant because he loves ignorance, and chooses ignorant thoughts; a man becomes wise because he loves wisdom and chooses wise thoughts. No man is hindered by another; he is only hindered by himself. No man suffers because of another; he suffers only because of himself. By the noble Gateway of Pure Thought you can enter the highest Heaven; by the ignoble doorway of impure thought you can descend into the lowest hell.

Your mental attitude towards others will faithfully react upon yourself, and will manifest itself in every relation of your life. Every impure and selfish thought that you send out comes back to you in your circumstances in some form of suffering; every pure and unselfish thought returns to you in some form of blessedness. Your circumstances are effects of which the cause is inward and invisible. As the father-mother of your thoughts you are the maker of your state and condition. When you know yourself, you will perceive, that every event in your life is weighed in the faultless balance of equity. When you understand the law within your mind you will cease to regard yourself as the impotent and blind tool of circumstances, and will become the strong and seeing master.

8

EFFECT OF THOUGHT ON HEALTH AND BODY

The body is the servant of the mind. It obeys the operations of the mind, whether they be deliberately chosen or automatically expressed. At the bidding of unlawful thoughts the body sinks rapidly into disease and decay; at the command of glad and beautiful thoughts it becomes clothed with youthfulness and beauty.

Disease and health, like circumstances, are rooted in thought. Sickly thoughts will express themselves through a sickly body. Thoughts of fear have been known to kill a man as speedily as a bullet, and they are continually killing thousands of people just as surely though less rapidly. The people who live in fear of disease are the people who get it. Anxiety quickly demoralizes the whole body, and lays it open to the, entrance of disease; while impure thoughts, even if not physically indulged, will soon shatter the nervous system.

Strong, pure, and happy thoughts build up the body in vigour and grace. The body is a delicate and plastic instrument, which responds readily to the thoughts by which it is impressed, and habits of thought will produce their own effects, good or bad, upon it.

Men will continue to have impure and poisoned blood, so long as they propagate unclean thoughts. Out of a clean heart comes a clean life and a clean body. Out of a defiled mind proceeds a defiled life and a corrupt body. Thought is the fount of action, life, and manifestation; make the fountain pure, and all will be pure.

Change of diet will not help a man who will not change his thoughts. When a man makes his thoughts pure, he no longer desires impure food.

Clean thoughts make clean habits. The so-called saint who does not wash his body is not a saint. He who has strengthened and purified his thoughts does not need to consider the malevolent microbe.

REJUVENATING THE BODY AND THE MIND

If you would protect your body, guard your mind. If you would renew your body, beautify your mind. Thoughts of malice, envy, disappointment, despondency, rob the body of its health and grace. A sour face does not come by chance; it is made by sour thoughts. Wrinkles that mar are drawn by folly, passion, and pride.

I know a woman of ninety-six who has the bright, innocent face of a girl. I know a man well under middle age whose face is drawn into inharmonious contours. The one is the result of a sweet and sunny disposition; the other is the outcome of passion and discontent.

As you cannot have a sweet and wholesome abode unless you admit the air and sunshine freely into your rooms, so a strong body and a bright, happy, or serene countenance can only result from the free admittance into the mind of thoughts of joy and goodwill and serenity.

On the faces of the aged there are wrinkles made by sympathy, others by strong and pure thought, and others are carved by passion: who cannot distinguish them? With those who have lived righteously, age is calm, peaceful, and softly mellowed, like the setting sun. I have recently seen a philosopher on his deathbed. He was not old except in years. He died as sweetly and peacefully as he had lived.

There is no physician like cheerful thought for dissipating the ills of the body; there is no comforter to compare with goodwill for dispersing the shadows of grief and sorrow. To live continually in thoughts of ill will, cynicism, suspicion, and envy, is to be confined in a self made prison-hole. But to think well of all, to be cheerful with all, to patiently learn to find the good in all—such unselfish thoughts are the very portals of heaven; and to dwell day by day in thoughts of peace toward every creature will bring abounding peace to their possessor.

9

LIGHT ON THE BLESSING AND DIGNITY OF WORK

That "labor is life" is a principle pregnant with truth, and one which cannot be too often repeated or too closely studied and practiced. Labor is so often regarded as an irksome and even degrading means of obtaining ease and pleasure, and not as what it really is—a thing happy and noble in itself. The lesson contained in the maxim needs to be taken to heart and more and more thoroughly learned.

Activity, both mental and physical, is the essence of life. The complete cessation of life is death, and death is immediately followed by corruption. Ease and death are closely related. The more there is of activity, the more abounding is life. The brainworker, the original thinker, the man of unceasing mental activity, is the longest-lived man in a community. The agricultural laborer, the gardener, the man of unceasing physical activity comes next with length in years.

Pure-hearted, healthy-minded people love work, and are happy in their labors. They never complain of being "overworked." It is very difficult, almost impossible, for a man to be overworked if he lives a sound and pure life. It is worry, bad habits, discontent and idleness that kill—especially idleness, for if labor is life, then idleness must be death. Let us get rid of sin before we talk about being overworked.

There are those who are afraid of work, regarding it as an enemy, and who fear a breakdown by doing too much. They have to learn what a health-bestowing friend work is. Others are ashamed of work, looking upon it as a degrading thing to be avoided. The "pure in heart and sound in head" are neither afraid nor ashamed of work, and they dignify whatsoever they undertake. No necessary work can be degrading, but if a man regards his work as such, he is already degraded, not by his task, but by his slavish vanity.

Man hath his daily work of body and mind Appointed, which declares his dignity.

The idle man who is afraid of work, and the vain man who is ashamed of it, are both on the way to poverty, if they are not already there. The industrious man, who loves work, and the man of true dignity, who glorifies work, are both on their way to affluence, if they are not already there. The lazy man is sowing the seeds of poverty and crime; the vain man is sowing the seeds of humiliation and shame. The industrious man is sowing the seeds of affluence and virtue; the dignified worker is sowing the seeds of victory and honor. Deeds are seeds, and the harvest will appear in due season.

There is a common desire to acquire riches with as little effort as possible, which is a kind of theft. To try to obtain the fruits of labor without laboring is to take the fruits of another man's labor; to try to get money without giving its equivalent is to take that which belongs to another and not one's self. What is theft but this frame of mind carried to its logical extreme?

Let us rejoice in our work. Let us rejoice that we have the strength and capacity for work, and let us increase that strength and capacity by unremitting labor.

Whatever our work may be, it is noble, and will be perceived by the world as noble, if we perform it with a noble spirit. The virtuous do not despise any labor which falls on their lot. And he who works and faints not, who is faithful, patient, and uncompromising even in the time of poverty, he will surely at last eat of the sweet fruits of his labor. Yea, even while he labors and seems to fail, happiness will be his constant companion, for, "Blessed is the man that has found his work; let him ask no other blessedness."

10

SMALL TASKS AND DUTIES

"Wrapped in our nearest duty is the key
Which shall unlock for us the Heavenly Gate:
Unveiled, the Heavenly Vision he shall see,
Who cometh not too early nor too late."

"Like the star
That shines afar,
Without haste
And without rest,

Let each man wheel with steady sway
Round the task that rules the day,
And do his best."

—Goethe

As pain and bliss inevitably follow on wrong and right beginnings, so unhappiness and blessedness are inseparably bound up with small tasks and duties. Not that a duty has any power of itself to bestow happiness or the reverse—this is contained in the attitude of the mind which is assumed towards the duty—and everything depends upon the way in which it is approached and done.

Not only great happiness but great power arises from doing

little things unselfishly, wisely, and perfectly, for life in its totality is made up of little things. Wisdom inheres in the common details of everyday existence, and when the parts are made perfect the Whole will be without blemish.

Everything in the universe is made up of little things, and the perfection of the great is based upon the perfection of the small. If any detail of the universe were imperfect the Whole would be imperfect. If any particle were omitted the aggregate would cease to be. Without a grain of dust there could be no world, and the world is perfect because the grain of dust is perfect. Neglect of the small is confusion of the great. The snowflake is as perfect as the star; the dew drop is as symmetrical as the planet; the microbe is not less mathematically proportioned than the man. By laying stone upon stone, plumbing and fitting each with perfect adjustment, the temple at last stands forth in all its architectural beauty. The small precedes the great. The small is not merely the apologetic attendant of the great, it is its master and informing genius.

Vain men are ambitious to be great, and look about to do some great thing, ignoring and despising the little tasks which call for immediate attention, and in the doing of which there is no vainglory, regarding such "trivialities" as beneath the notice of great men. The fool lacks knowledge because he lacks humility, and, inflated with the thought of self-importance, he aims at impossible things.

The great man has become such by the scrupulous and unselfish attention which he has given to small duties. He has become wise and powerful by sacrificing ambition and pride in the doing of those necessary things which evoke no applause and promise no reward. He never sought greatness; he sought faithfulness, unselfishness, integrity, truth; and in finding these in the common round of small tasks and duties he unconsciously ascended to the level of greatness.

The great man knows the vast value that inheres in moments, words, greetings, meals, apparel, correspondence, rest, work, detached efforts, fleeting obligations, in the thousand-and-one little things which press upon him for attention—briefly, in the common details of life. He sees everything as divinely apportioned, needing only the application of dispassionate thought and action on his part to render life blessed and perfect. He neglects nothing; does not hurry; seeks to escape nothing but error and folly; attends to every duty as it is presented to him, and does not postpone and regret. By giving himself unreservedly to his nearest duty, forgetting alike pleasure and pain, he attains to that combined childlike simplicity and unconscious power which is greatness.

The advice of Confucius to his disciples: "Eat at your own table as you would at the table of a king," emphasises the immeasurable importance of little things, as also does that aphorism of another great teacher, Buddha: "If anything is to be done, let a man do it, let him attack it vigorously." To neglect small tasks, or to execute them in a perfunctory or slovenly manner, is a mark of weakness and folly.

The giving of one's entire and unselfish attention to every duty in its proper place evolves, by a natural growth, higher and ever higher combinations of duties, because it evolves power and develops talent, genius, goodness, character. A man ascends into greatness as naturally and unconsciously as the plant evolves a flower, and in the same manner, by fitting, with unabated energy and diligence, every effort and detail in its proper place, Thus, harmonising his life and character without friction or waste of power.

Of the almost innumerable recipes for the development of "will-power" and "concentration" which are now scattered abroad, one looks almost in vain for any wholesome hint applicable to vital experience. "Breathings," "postures," "visualisings," "occult methods" are practices as delusive as they are artificial and remote from all that is real and essential in life; while the true path—the path of duty, of earnest and undivided application to one's daily task—along which alone will-power and concentration of thought can be wholesomely and normally developed, remains unknown, untrodden, unexplored even by the elect.

All unnatural forcing and straining in order to gain "power" should be abandoned. There is no way from childhood to manhood but by growth; nor is there any other way from folly to wisdom, from ignorance to knowledge, from weakness to strength. A man must learn how to grow little by little and day after day, by adding thought to thought, effort to effort, deed to deed.

It is true the fakir gains some sort of power by his long persistence in "postures" and "mortifications," but it is a power which is bought at a heavy price, and that price is an equal loss of strength in another direction. He is never a strong, useful character, but a mere fantastic specialist in some psychological trick. He is not a developed man, he is a maimed man.

LESS IS MORE

True will-power consists in overcoming the irritabilities, follies, rash impulses and moral lapses which accompany the daily life of the individual, and which are apt to manifest themselves on every slight provocation; and in developing calmness, self-possession, and dispassionate action in the press and heat of worldly duties, and in the midst of the passionate and unbalanced throng. Anything short of this is not true power, and this can only be developed along the normal pathway of steady growth in executing ever more and more masterfully, unselfishly, and perfectly the daily round of legitimate tasks and pressing obligations.

The master is not he whose "psychological accomplishments," rounded by mystery and wonder, leave him in unguarded moments the prey of irritability, of regret, of peevishness, or other petty folly or vice, but he whose "mastery" is manifested in fortitude, non-resentment, steadfastness, calmness, and infinite patience. The true Master is master of himself; anything other than this is not mastery but delusion. The man who sets his whole mind on the doing of each task as it is presented, who puts into it energy and intelligence, shutting all else out from his mind, and striving to do that one thing, no matter how small, completely and perfectly, detaching himself from all reward in his task—that man will every day be acquiring greater command over his mind, and will, by ever-ascending degrees, become at last a man of power—a Master.

Put yourself unreservedly into your present task, and so work, so act, so live that you shall leave each task a finished piece of labour—this is the true way to the acquisition of will-power, concentration of thought, and conservation of energy. Look not about for magical formulas, for strained and artificial methods. Every resource is already with you and within you. You have but to learn how wisely to apply yourself in that place which you now occupy. Until this is done those other and higher places which are waiting for you cannot be taken possession of, cannot be reached.

There is no way to strength and wisdom but by acting strongly and wisely in the present moment, and each present moment reveals its own task. The great man, the wise man does small things greatly regarding nothing as "trivial" that is necessary. The weak man, the foolish man, does small things carelessly, and meanly, hankering the while after, some greater work for which, in his neglect and inability in small matters, he is ceaselessly advertising his incapacity. The man who leasts governs himself is always more ambitious to govern others and assume important responsibilities. "Who so neglects a thing which he suspects he ought to do because it seems too small a thing is deceiving himself; it is not too little but too great for him that he doeth it not."

And just as the strong doing of small tasks leads to greater strength, so the doing of those tasks weakly leads to greater weakness. What a man is in his fractional duties that he is in the aggregate of his character. Weakness is as great a source of suffering as sin, and there can be no true blessedness until some measure of strength of character is evolved. The weak man becomes strong by attaching value to little things and doing them accordingly. The strong man becomes weak by falling into looseness and neglect concerning small things, thereby forfeiting his simple wisdom and squandering his energy. Herein we see the beneficent operation of that law of growth which is expressed in the little understood words: "To him that hath shall be given, and from him that hath not shall be taken away even that which he hath." Man instantly gains or loses by every thought he thinks, every word he says, every act he does, and every work to which he puts hand and heart. His character from moment to moment is a graduating quantity, to or from which some measure of good is added or subtracted during every moment, and the gain or loss is involved, even to absoluteness, in each thought, word, and deed as these follow each other in rapid sequence.

He who masters the small becomes the rightful possessor of the great. He who is mastered by the small can achieve no superlative victory.

Life is a kind of cooperative trust in which the whole is of the nature of, and dependent upon, the unit.

A successful business, a perfect machine, a glorious temple, or a beautiful character is evolved from the perfect adjustment of a multiplicity of parts.

The foolish man thinks that little faults, little indulgences, little sins, are of no consequence; he persuades himself that so long as he does not commit flagrant immoralities he is virtuous, and even holy; but he is thereby deprived of virtue, and holiness, and the world knows him accordingly; it does not reverence, adore, and love him; it passes him by; he is reckoned of no account; his influence is destroyed. The efforts of such a man to make the world virtuous, his exhortations to his fellow-men to abandon great vices, are empty of substance and barren of fruitage. The insignificance which he attaches to his small vices permeates his whole character and is the measure of his manhood: he is regarded as an insignificant man. The levity with which he commits his errors and publishes his weakness comes back to him in the form of neglect and loss of influence and respect: he is not sought after, for who will seek to be taught of folly? His work does not prosper, for who will lean upon a reed? His words fall upon deaf ears, for they are void of practice, wisdom, and experience, and who will go after an echo?

The wise man, or he who is becoming wise, sees the danger which lurks in those common personal faults which men mostly commit thoughtlessly and with impunity; he also sees the salvation which inheres in the abandonment of those faults, as well as in the practice of virtuous thoughts and acts which the majority disregard as unimportant, and in those quiet but momentous daily conquests over self which are hidden from other's eyes.

He who regards his molest delinquencies as of the gravest nature becomes a saint. He sees the far reaching influence, good or bad, which extends from his every thought and act, and how he himself is made or unmade by the soundness or unsoundness of those innumerable details of conduct which combine to form his character and life, and so he watches, guards, purifies, and perfects himself little by little and step by step.

As the ocean is composed of drops, the earth of grains, and the stars of points of light, so is life composed of thoughts and acts; without these, life would not be. Every man's life, therefore, is what his apparently detached thoughts and acts make it. There combination is himself. As the year consists, of a given number of sequential moments, so a man's character and life consists of a given number of sequential thoughts and deeds, and the finished whole will bear the impress of the parts.

"All sorts of things and weather
Must be taken in together,
To make up a year
And a sphere."

Little kindnesses, generosities, and sacrifices make up a kind and generous character. Little renunciations, endurances, and victories over self make up a strong and noble character. The truly honest man is honest in the minutest details of his life. The noble man is noble in every little thing he says and does.

It is a fatal delusion with men to think that life is detached from the momentary thought and act, and not to understand that the passing thought and deed is the foundation and substance of life. When this is fully understood all things are seen as sacred, and every act becomes religious. Truth is wrapped up in infinitesimal details. Thoroughness is genius.

> "Possessions vanish, and opinions change,
> And passions hold a fluctuating seat:
> But, by the storms of circumstance unshaken,
> And subject neither to eclipse nor wane,
> Duty exists."

You do not live your life in the mass; you live it in the fragments and from these the mass emerges. You can will to live each fragment nobly if you choose, and, this being done, there can be no particle of baseness in the finished whole. The saying "Take care of the pence and the pounds will take care of themselves" is seen to be more than worldly-wise when applied spiritually, for, to take care of the present, passing act, knowing that by so doing the total sum and amount of life and character will be safely preserved, is to be divinely wise. Do not long to do great and laudable things; these will do themselves if you do your present task nobly. Do not chafe at the restrictions and limitations of your present duty but be nobly unselfish in the doing of it, putting aside discontent, listlessness, and the foolish contemplation of great deeds which lie beyond you—and lo! already the greatness for which you sighed begins to appear. There is no weakness like peevishness. Aspire to the attainment of inward nobility, not outward glory, and begin to attain it where you now are.

The irksomeness and sting which you feel to be in your task are in your mind only. Alter your attitude of mind towards it, and at once the crooked path is made straight, the unhappiness is turned into joy.

See that your every fleeting moment is strong, pure, and purposeful; put earnestness and unselfishness into every passing task and duty; make your every thought, word, and deed sweet and true; Thus, learning, by practice and experience, the inestimable value of the small things of life, you will gather, little by little, abundant and enduring blessedness.

11

THE JOY OF ACCOMPLISHMENT

Joy is always the accompaniment of a task successfully accomplished. An undertaking completed, or a piece of work done, always brings rest and satisfaction. "When a man has done his duty, he is light-hearted and happy," says Emerson; and no matter how insignificant the task may appear, the doing of it faithfully and with whole-souled energy always results in cheerfulness and peace of mind.

Of all miserable men, the shirker is the most miserable. Thinking to find ease and happiness in avoiding difficult duties and necessary tasks, which require the expenditure of labor and exertion, his mind is always uneasy and disturbed, he becomes burdened with an inward sense of shame, and forfeits manliness and self-respect.

"He who will not work according to his faculty, let him perish according to his necessity," says Carlyle; and it is a moral law that the man who avoids duty, and does not work to the full extent of his capacity, does actually perish, first in his character and last in his body and circumstances. Life and action are synonymous, and immediately a man tries to escape exertion, either physical or mental, he has commenced to decay.

On the other hand, the energetic increase in life by the full exercise of their powers, by overcoming difficulties, and by bringing to completion tasks which coiled for the strenuous use of mind or muscle.

How happy is a child when a school lesson, long labored over, is mastered at last! The athlete, who has trained his body through long months or years of discipline and strain, is richly blessed in his increased health and strength; and is met with the rejoicings of his friends when he carries home the prize from the field of contest. After many years of ungrudging toil, the heart of the scholar is gladdened with the advantages and powers which learning bestows.

The business man, grappling incessantly with difficulties and drawbacks, is amply repaid in the happy assurance of well earned success; and the horticulturist, vigorously contending with the stubborn soil, sits down at last to eat of the fruits of his labor.

INEVITABILITY OF FAILURE

Every successful accomplishment, even in worldly things, is repaid with its own measure of joy; and in spiritual things, the joy which supervenes upon the perfection of purpose is sure, deep and abiding. Great is the heartfelt joy (albeit ineffable) when, after innumerable and apparently unsuccessful attempts, some ingrained fault of character is at last cast out to trouble its erstwhile victim and the world no more.

The striver after virtue—he who is engaged in the holy task of building up a noble character—tastes, at every step of conquest over self, a joy which does not again leave him, but which becomes an integral part of his spiritual nature.

All life is a struggle; both without and within there are conditions against which man must contend; his very existence is a series of efforts and accomplishments, and his right to remain among men as a useful unit of humanity depends upon the measure of his capacity for wrestling successfully with the elements of nature without, or with the enemies of virtue and truth within.

It is demanded of man that he shall continue to strive after better things, after greater perfection, after higher and still higher achievements; and in accordance with the measure of his obedience to this demand, does the angel of joy wait upon his footsteps and minister unto him; for he who is anxious to learn, eager to know, and who puts forth efforts to accomplish, finds the joy which eternally sings at the heart of the universe.

First in little things, then in greater, and then in greater still, must man strive; until at last he is prepared to make the supreme effort, and strive for the accomplishment of Truth, succeeding in which, he will realize the eternal joy.

The price of life is effort; the acme of effort is accomplishment; the reward of accomplishment is joy. Blessed is the man who strives against his own selfishness; he will taste in its fullness the joy of accomplishment.

12

MEMORY, REPETITION, AND HABIT

I shall gain.
By purity and strong self-mastery,
The awakened vision that doth set men free
From painful slumber and the night of grief.

When a particular combination of words has been repeated a number of times, it is said to have been committed to memory—that is, it can then be repeated without visual reference to the words themselves, and without pause or effort; indeed, the words have then a tendency to repeat themselves in the mind, and sometimes people are troubled with the ringing of a refrain, or the repetition of a sentence in the mind, which they find it very difficult to get rid of and forget.

There is a sense in which the whole of life is a process of committing to memory. At first there is *act,* from act springs *experience,* from experience arises *recollection,* from recollection *repetition,* and from repetition is formed *habit*; hence proceeds impulse, faculty, character, individualised existence.

Life is a repetition of the same things over again. There is very little difference between the days and years in the life of a man; one is almost entirely a repetition of the other. Every being is an accumulation of experiences gathered, learnt, and woven into the life by a ceaseless series of repetitions extending over an incalculable number of lives which thread their way through eons of time.

The life of a man, from the germ-cell to maturity, is a repetition, in synthesis, of the entire process of evolution. There is a cosmic memory at the root of all growth and progress, which is an informing and sustaining principle in the process of evolution.

The sensuous memory of man is fickle and ephemeral, but the supersensuous memory which is inherent in all matter, building up forms and faculty is infallible in its reproduction of experiences.

Life is ceaseless reiteration. Nature ever travels over old and familiar ground. Man is daily repeating that which he has learnt though: the schools of experience in which the lessons were acquired may be long forgotten; but the acquired habit is not forgotten; it is carried forward and continues to act. The unconscious and automatic ease which marks the play of faculty is not the ready-made mechanism of an arbitrary creator; it is *skill acquired by practice;* it is the consummation of millions of repetitions of. the same thought and act.

Thoughts and deeds long persisted in become at last spontaneous impulses.

It is a profound truth that "there is nothing new under the sun." It is possible and highly probable that, in the round of eternity, even all our modern inventions and mechanical marvels have been produced innumerable times on this or other worlds. In this world, new combinations of matter appear from time to time, but are they new in the universe? Who dare say that, in the mind which overarches eternity, the cosmic memory is not reproducing things long since fashioned out of itself?

Nothing can be added to, or taken from, the universe. Its matter can neither be increased nor decreased. Chemical combinations of matter vary, but matter itself cannot vary. Life likewise does not change. In the forms of life there is continuous flux, but in the principle of life there is no increase or diminution. Forms come forth only to retreat and disappear; but that which disappears is not lost; the memory of it is retained, and it continues to be repeated. Eternal disintegration is balanced by eternal restitution.

The mind of man is not separate from the Eternal Mind; in its daily repetitions is indelibly written the record of all its past. *Character is an accumulation of deeds.* Each man is the last reckoning in the long sum of evolution, and there is no falsification of the account. The mind continues to automatically perform the habit which encloses a million repetitions of the same deed. Compared with this ineffaceable, unconscious memory, the memory of three score years and ten is as a fading vapour to an Egyptian Pyramid. The tendencies, impulses, and habits of which a man is a victim are the repetitions of his accumulated deeds. They enfold the destiny which he has wrought. The grace, goodness, and genius which a man exhibits without conscious effort are the fruits of the accumulated labours of his mind. He repeats with ease that which was learned by painful labour. The wise man sees a reflection of himself in the fate which overtakes him.

Life flows in channels. Every man is in a rut. Men tell their fellows to "get out of their ruts," but they themselves are in ruts of another kind. The flow of law, of nature, cannot be avoided, but it can be utilised. We cannot avoid ruts, but we can avoid bad ones; we can follow along good ones.

In their training and education, the children of to-day are

strictly confined to ways which are worn by the feet of a thousand generations. In his fixed habits and characteristics, the man of to-day is reviving the actions of a thousand lives.

It is true that men are bound; but it is equally true that they can unbind. The law by which a man becomes the sorrowful victim of his own wrong deeds is a blessed, and not a cursed, law; for by the same law he can become the instrument of all that is good. Habits chain a man, but he himself forged the links. He whose inner eye has opened to perceive the law does not complain. The bondage of evil is a heavy slavery, but the bondage of good is a blessed service.

The will of man is powerless to alter the law of life, but it is powerful to obey it. The Great Law makes for good; it puts a heavy penalty on evil. Man can break his chains, and shake himself free; and when he enters earnestly upon the work of self-liberation, all the universe will be with him in his labour. Repetition and habit he cannot avoid, but he can set going repetitions that are harmonious, he can form habits that will crystallise into pure and noble characteristics.

In the self-built archives of the mind are stored away the entire records of man's evolution. Man is an epitomised history of the world. In his outbursts of rage we hear again the roar of the lion in the forest; in his selfish schemings to secure his coveted ends we see the tiger stalking its prey; his lusts, revenges, hatreds, and fears are the instinct born of primeval experiences. The universe does not forget; life remembers and restores.

Between the sensuous and the supersensuous worlds is the Lethean stream, the river of forgetfulness. Only he who has passed into the supersensuous world—the world of pure goodness—remembers with the Memory of Life which transcends a million deaths. Only he whose will obeys the Universal Will, whose heart is,in harmony with the Cosmic Order, receives the vision which pierces through the vale of time and matter, and sees the before and the beyond.

Man quickly forgets, and it is well that he forgets; the universe remembers and records. The repetition of an evil deed is its own retribution; the repetition of a good deed is its own reward. The deepest punishment of evil is evil; the highest reward of good is good. When a deed is done, it is not ended; it is but begun; it remains with the doer—to curse him, if evil; to bless him, if good. Deeds accumulate by repetition, and they remain as character, and in character is both curse and blessing.

Suffering inheres in the discordant repetition of evil; bliss inheres in the rhythmic repetitions of good. Seeing that we cannot escape the law of repetition, let us choose to do those things which are good; and as one establishes habits of purity, the divine memory will be awakened within him.

13

DOING AND KNOWING

Let a man realize that his life, in its totality, proceeds from his mind. Let him realize that the mind is a combination of habits which he can, by patient effort, modify to any extent, and over which he can Thus, gain complete ascendancy, mastery, and control. At once, he will have obtained possession of the key which shall open the door to his complete emancipation.

But freedom from the ills of life (which are the ills of one's mind) is a matter of steady growth from within, and not a sudden acquisition from without. Hourly and daily must the mind be trained to think stainless thoughts, and adapt right and dispassionate attitudes under those circumstances in which it is prone to fall into wrong and passion. Like the patient sculptor upon his marble, the aspirant to the Right Life must gradually work upon the crude material of his mind until he has wrought out of it the Ideal of his holiest dreams.

In working toward such supreme accomplishment, it is necessary to begin at the lowest and easiest steps, and proceed by natural, progressive stages to the higher and more difficult. This law of growth, progress, evolution, and unfoldment, by gradual and ever ascending stages, is absolute in every department of life, and in every human accomplishment. Where it is ignored, total failure will result.

In acquiring education, in learning a trade, or in pursuing

a business, this law is fully recognized and minutely obeyed by all. But in acquiring Virtue, in learning Truth, and in pursuing the right conduct and knowledge of life, it is unrecognized and disobeyed by nearly all. Hence Virtue, Truth, and the Perfect Life remain unpracticed, unacquired, and unknown.

It is a common error to suppose that the Higher Life is a matter of reading, and the adoption of theological or metaphysical hypotheses, and that Spiritual Principles can be understood by this method. The Higher Life is higher living in thought, word, and deed, and the knowledge of those Spiritual Principles which are imminent in man and in the universe can only be acquired after long discipline in the pursuit and practice of Virtue.

The lesser must be thoroughly grasped and understood before the greater can be known. Practice always precedes real knowledge.

The schoolmaster never attempts to teach his pupils the abstract principles of mathematics at the start. He knows that such a method of teaching would be in vain, and learning impossible. He first places before them a simple sum, and, having explained it, leaves them to do it. When, after repeated failures and ever renewed effort, they have succeeded in doing it correctly, a more difficult task is set before them, and then another and another. It is not until the pupils have, through many years of diligent application, mastered all the lessons in arithmetic, that he attempts to unfold to them the underlying mathematical principles.

In learning a trade, say that of a mechanic, a boy is not at first taught the principles of mechanics, but a simple tool is put in his hand and he is told how rightly to use it. He is then left to do it by effort and practice. As he succeeds in plying his tools correctly, more and more difficult tasks are set before him, until after several years of successful practice, he is prepared to study and grasp the principles of mechanics.

In a properly governed household, the child is first taught to be obedient, and to conduct himself properly under all circumstances. The child is not even told why he must do this, but is commanded to do it. Only after he has far succeeded in doing what is right and proper, is he told why he should do it. No father would attempt to teach his child the principles of ethics before exacting from him the practice of family duty and social virtue.

Thus, practice ever precedes knowledge even in the ordinary things of the world, and in spiritual things, in the living of the Higher Life, this law is rigid in its demands.

Virtue can only be known by doing, and the knowledge of Truth can only be arrived at by perfecting oneself in the practice of Virtue. To be complete in the practice and acquisition of Virtue is to be complete in the knowledge of Truth.

Truth can only be arrived at by daily and hourly doing the lessons of Virtue, beginning with the simplest, and passing on to the more difficult. A child patiently and obediently learns his lessons at school by constantly practicing, ever exerting himself until all failures and difficulties are surmounted. Likewise does the child of Truth, undaunted by failure, and made stronger by difficulties, apply himself to rightdoing in thought and action. As he succeeds in acquiring Virtue, his mind unfolds itself in the knowledge of Truth, and it is a knowledge in which he can securely rest.

14

TEMPTATION

Aspiration can carry a man into heaven, but to remain there, he must learn to conform his entire mind to the heavenly conditions. To this end temptation works.

Temptation is the reversion, in thought, from purity to passion. It is going back from aspiration to desire. It threatens aspiration until the point is reached where desire is quenched in the waters of pure knowledge and calm thought.

In the early stages of aspiration, temptation is subtle and powerful, and is regarded as an enemy; but it is only an enemy in the sense that the one tempted is his own enemy. In the sense that it is the revealer of weakness and impurity, it is a friend, a necessary factor in spiritual training. It is, indeed, an accompaniment of the effort to overcome evil and apprehend good. To be successfully conquered, the evil in a man must come to the surface and present itself, and it is in temptation that the evil hidden in the heart stands revealed and exposed.

That which temptation appeals to and arouses is unconquered desire, and temptation will again and again assail a man until he has lifted himself above the lusting impulses. Temptation is an appeal to the impure. That which is pure cannot be subject to temptation.

Temptation waylays the man of aspiration until he touches the region of the divine consciousness, and beyond that border temptation cannot follow him. It is when a man begins to aspire that he begins to be tempted. Aspiration rouses up all the latent good and evil, in order that the man may be fully revealed to himself, for a man cannot overcome himself unless he fully knows himself.

It can scarcely be said of the merely animal man that he is tempted, for the very presence of temptation means that there is a striving for a purer state. Animal desire and gratification is the normal condition of the man who has not yet risen into aspiration. He wishes for nothing more, nothing better, than his sensual enjoyments, and is, for the present, satisfied. Such a man cannot be tempted to fall, for he has not yet risen.

The presence of aspiration signifies that a man has taken one step, at least, upward, and is therefore capable of being drawn back. This backward attraction is called temptation. The allurements of temptation subsist in the impure thoughts and downward desires of the heart. The object of temptation is powerless to attract when the heart no longer lusts for it. The stronghold of temptation is within a man, not without; and until a man realizes this, the period of temptation will be prolonged.

While a man continues to run away from outward objects, under the delusion that temptation subsists entirely in them, and does not attack and purge away his impure imaginings, his temptations will increase, and his falls will be many and grievous. When a man clearly perceives that the evil is within and not without, then his progress will be rapid, his temptations will decrease, and the final overcoming of all temptation will be well within the range of his spiritual vision.

Temptation is torment. It is not an abiding condition, but is a passage from a lower condition to a higher. The fullness and perfection of life is bliss, not torment. Temptation accompanies weakness and defeat, but a man is destined for strength and victory. The presence of torment is the signal to rise and conquer. The man of persistent and ever renewed aspiration does not allow himself to think that temptation cannot be overcome. He is determined to be master of himself. Resignation to evil is an acknowledgment of defeat. It signifies that the battle against self is abandoned; that good is denied; that evil is made supreme.

As the energetic man of business is not daunted by difficulties but studies how to overcome them, so the man of ceaseless aspiration is not crushed into submission by temptations, but meditates how he may fortify his mind. For the tempter is like a coward: he only creeps in at weak and unguarded points.

The tempted one should study thoughtfully the nature and meaning of temptation, for until it is known it cannot be overcome. A wise general, before attacking the opposing force, studies the tactics of his enemy. Likewise, he who is to overcome temptation must understand how it arises in his own darkness and error, and must study, by introspection and meditation, how to disperse the darkness and supplant error by truth.

The stronger a man's passions, the fiercer will be his temptations; the deeper his selfishness, the more subtle his temptations; the more pronounced his vanity, the more flattering and deceptive his temptations.

A man must know himself if he is to know the truth. He must not shrink from any revelation which will expose his error. On the contrary, he must welcome such revelations as aids to that self-knowledge which is the handmaid of self-conquest.

The man who cannot endure to have his errors and shortcomings brought to the surface and made known, but tries to hide them, is unfit to walk the highway of truth. He is not properly equipped to battle with and overcome temptation.

He who cannot fearlessly face his lower nature, cannot climb the rugged heights of renunciation.

Foolish men blame others for their lapses and sins, but let the truth-lover blame only himself. Let him acknowledge his complete responsibility for his own conduct and not say, when he falls, this thing, or such and such a circumstance, or that man was to blame. For the most which others can do is to afford an opportunity for our own good or evil to manifest itself. They cannot make us good or evil.

Temptation is at first sore, grievous, and hard to be borne, and subtle and persistent is the assailant. But if the tempted one is firm and courageous, and does not give way, he will gradually subdue his spiritual enemy, and will finally triumph in the knowledge of good.

The adverse one is compounded of a man's own lust, selfishness, and pride. When these are put away, evil is seen to be naught, and good is revealed in all-victorious splendor.

15

THE SHINING GATEWAY OF MEDITATION

Be watchful, fearless, faithful, patient, pure:
By earnest meditation sound the depths
Profound of life, and scale the heights sublime
Of Love and Wisdom. He who does not find
The Way of Meditation cannot reach
Emancipation and enlightenment.

The unregenerate man is subject to these three things—*Desire, Passion, Sorrow.* He lives habitually in these conditions, and neither questions nor examines them. He regards them as his life itself, and cannot conceive of any life apart from them. To-day he desires, to-morrow he indulges his passions, and the third day he grieves; by these three things (which are always found together) he is impelled, and does not know why he is so impelled; the inner forces of desire and passion arise, almost automatically, within him, and he gratifies their demands *Sans* question; led on blindly by his blind desires, he falls, periodically, into the ditches of remorse and sorrow. His condition is not merely unintelligible to him, it is unperceived: for so immersed is he in the desire (or self) consciousness that he cannot step outside of it, as it were, to examine it.

To such a man the idea of rising above desire and suffering into a new life where such things do not obtain seems ridiculous. He associates all life with *the pleasurable gratification of desire,* and so, by the law of reaction, he also lives in the misery of afflictions, fluctuating ceaselessly between pleasure and pain.

When reflection dawns in the mind, there arises a sense (dim and uncertain at first) of a calmer, wiser, and loftier life; and as the stages of introspection and self-analysis are reached, this sense increases in clearness and intensity, so that by the time the first three stages are fully completed, a conviction of the reality of such a life and of the possibility of attaining it is firmly fixed in the mind.

Such conviction, which consists of a steadfast belief in the supremacy of purity and goodness over desire and passion, is called *faith.* Such faith is the stay, support and comfort of the man who, while yet in the darkness, is searching earnestly for the Light which breaks upon him for the first time in all its dazzling splendour and ineffable majesty when he enters the Shining Gateway of Meditation. Without such faith he could not stand for a single day against the trials, failures, and difficulties which beset him continually, much less could be courageously fight and overcome them, and his final conquest and salvation would be impossible.

Upon entering the stage of meditation, faith gradually ripens into knowledge, and the new regenerate life begins to be realised in its quiet wisdom, calm beauty, and ordered strength, and day by day its joy and splendour increase.

The final conquest over sin is now assured. Lust, hatred, anger, covetousness, pride and vanity, desire for pleasure, wealth, and fame, worldly honour and power –all these have become dead things, shortly to pass away forever; there is no more life nor happiness in them; they have no part in the life of the regenerate one, who knows that he can never again go back to them, for now the "Old man" of self and sin is dead, and the "new man" of Love and Purity is born within him. He has become (or becomes, as the process of meditation ripens and bears fruit) a new being, one in whom Purity, Love, Wisdom, and Peacefulness are the ruling qualities, and wherein strifes, envies, suspicions, hatreds, and jealousies cannot find lodgment. "Old things have passed away, and, behold, all things have become new"; men and things are seen in a different light, and a new universe is unveiled; there is no confusion; as out of the inner chaos of conflicting desires, passions, and sufferings the new being arises, there arises in the outer world of apparently irreconcilable conditions a new Cosmos, ordered, sequential, harmonious, ineffably glorious, faultless in equity.

Meditation is a process both of *Purification* and *Adjustment.* Aspiration is the purifying element, and the harmonising power resides in the intellectual train of thought involved.

When the stage of meditation is reached and entered upon, two distinct processes of spiritual transmutation is reached and entered upon, two distinct processes of spiritual transmutation begin to take place, namely:

1. Transmutation of passion.
2. Transmutation of affliction.

The two conditions proceed simultaneously, as they are interdependent, and act and react one upon the other. Passion and affliction, or sin and suffering, are two aspects of one thing, namely, the *Self* in man, that self which is the source of all the troubles which afflict mankind. They represent *Power*, but power wrongly used. Passion is a lower manifestation of a divine energy which possesses a higher use and application. Affliction is the limitation and negation of that energy, and is therefore a means of restoring harmony. "It says, in effect to the self-bound man, "Thus, far shalt thou go and no farther." The man of meditation transfers the passional energy from the realm of evil (Self-following) to the realm, of good (self-overcoming). To-day he reflects, tomorrow he overcomes his passions, and the third day he rejoices. The mind is drawn from its downward tendency, and is directed upwards. The base metal of error is transmuted into the pure gold of Truth. Lust, hatred, and selfishness disappear; and purity, love, and goodwill take their place. As the stage proceeds, the mind becomes more and more firmly fixed in the higher manifestations, and it becomes increasingly difficult for it to think and act in the lower; and just in the measure that the mind is freed from the lower, violent, and inharmonious activities, just so much is passion transmuted into power, and affliction into bliss.

This means that there is no such thing as affliction to the sinless man. When sin is put away, affliction disappears.

Selfhood is the source of suffering; Truth is the source of bliss.

When the unregenerate man is abused, or slandered, misunderstood, or persecuted, it causes him intense suffering; but when these things are brought to bear on the regenerate man, there arises in him the rapture of heavenly bliss. None but he who has put away the great enemy, self, under his feet can fully enter into and understand the saying:

> Blessed are ye, when men shall revile you, and persecute you, and shall say all manner of evil against you falsely, for my sake. Rejoice, and be exceeding glad.

And why does the righteous (regenerate) man rejoice under those conditions which cause such misery to the unrighteous (unregenerate) man? It is because, having overcome the evil in himself, he ceases to see evil without. To the good man all things are good, and he utilises everything for the good of the world. To him persecution is not an evil, it is a good. Having acquired insight, knowledge, and power, he, by meeting that persecution in a loving spirit, helps and uplifts his persecutors, and accelerates their spiritual progress, though they themselves know it not at the time. Thus, he is filled with unspeakable bliss because he has conquered the forces of evil; because, instead of succumbing to those forces, he has learned how to use and direct them for the good and gain of mankind. He is blessed because he is at one with all men, because he is reconciled to the universe, and has brought himself into harmony with the Cosmic Order.

The following symbol will perhaps help the mind of the reader to more readily grasp what has been explained.

LOVE, LIGHT, AND LIFE KNOWLEDGE

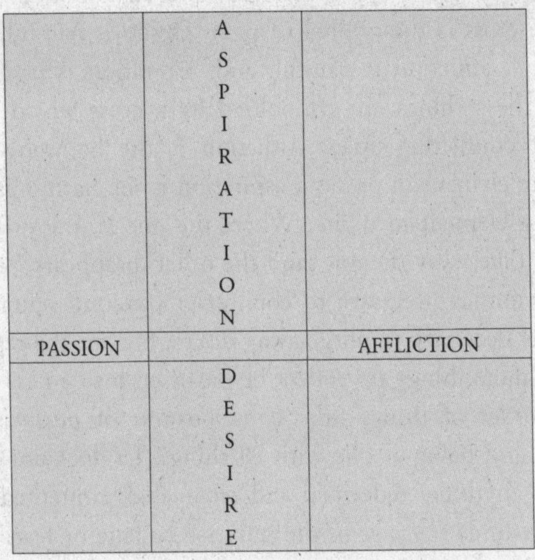

IGNORANCE LUST, DARKNESS AND DEATH

There is at first the underworld of *lust, darkness,* and *death* which is associated with ignorance; rooted in this is the foot of the cross—*desire*; in the body of the cross, desire branches out into two arms—the right (active or positive) are, *passion,* being equalised and balanced by the left (passive or negative) arm of affliction; uniting these, and rising out of them at the head of the cross, is aspiration; here, wounded and bleeding, rests the thorn-crowned head, of humanity; at the end of this, and right at the summit of the cross, *is knowledge,* which, while being at the apex of the self-life, is the base of the Truth-life; and above rises the heavenly world of *Love, Light,* and *Life.*

In this supremely beautiful world the regenerate man lives, even while living on this earth. He has reached Nirvana, the Kingdom of Heaven. He has taken up his cross, and there is no more sin and sufferings desire and passion and affliction are passed away. Harmony is restored, and all is bliss and peace.

The cross is the symbol of pain. Desire is painful, passion is painful, affliction is painful, and. aspiration is painful; this is why these things are symbolised by a cross which has two pairs of conflicting poles. Affliction is the harmonising and purifying element in passion; aspiration is the harmonising and purifying element in desire. Where the one is, the other must be also. Take away the one, and the other disappears. Suffering, or affliction, is necessary to counteract passion; aspiration, or prayer, is necessary to purge away desire; but for the regenerate man all these things are ended; he has-risen into a new life and a new order of things—the consciousness of purity; lacking nothing and being at one with all things, he does not need to pray for anything; redeemed and reconciled, contented and ill peace, he finds nothing in the universe to hate or fear, and his is both the duty and the power to work without ceasing for the present good and the ultimate salvation of mankind.

16

SOLITUDE

"Why idly seek from outward things
The answer inward silence brings?
Why climb the far-off hills with pain,
A nearer view of heaven to gain?
In lowliest depths of bosky dells
The hermit Contemplation dwells,
Whence, piercing heaven, with screened sight,
He sees at noon the stars, whose light
Shall glorify the coming night."

—Whittier

"In the still hour when passion is at rest
Gather up stores of wisdom in thy breast."

—Wordsworth

Man's essential being is inward, invisible, spiritual, and as such it derives its life, strength, from within, not from without. Outward things are channels through which its energies are expended, but for renewal it must fall back on the inward silence.

In so far as man strives to drown this silence in the noisy pleasures of the senses, and endeavours to live in the conflicts of outward things, just so much does he reap the experiences of pain and sorrow, which, becoming at last intolerable, drive him back to the feet of inward Comforter, to the shrine of the peaceful solitude within.

As the body cannot thrive on empty husks, neither can the spirit be sustained on empty pleasures. If not regularly fed the body loses its vitality, and, pained with hunger and thirst, cries out for food and drink. It is the same with the spirit: it must be regularly nourished in solitude on pure and holy thoughts or it will lose its freshness and strength, and will at last cry out in its painful and utter starvation. The yearning of an anguish-stricken soul for light and consolation is the cry of a spirit that is perishing of hunger and thirst. All pain and sorrow is spiritual starvation, and aspiration is the cry for food. It is the Prodigal Son who, perishing of hunger, turns his face longingly towards his Father's home.

The pure life of the spirit cannot be found; but is lost, in the life of the senses. The lower desires are ever clamorous for more, and they afford no rest. The outward world of pleasure, personal contact, and noisy activities is a sphere of wear and tear which necessitates the counterbalancing effect of solitude. Just as the body requires rest for the recuperation of its forces, so the spirit requires solitude for the renewal of its energies. Solitude is as indispensable to man's spiritual welfare as sleep is to his bodily well-being; and pure thought, or meditation, which is evoked in solitude, is to the spirit what activity is to the body. As the body breaks down when deprived of the needful rest and sleep, so do the spirits of men break down, being deprived of the necessary silence and solitude. Man, as a spiritual being, cannot be maintained in strength, uprightness, and peace except he periodically withdraws himself from the outer world of perishable things and reach inwardly towards the abiding and imperishable realities. The consolations of the creeds are derived from the solitude which those creeds enforce. The regular observance of the ceremonies of formal religion, attended, as they are, with concentrated silence and freedom from worldly distractions, compels men to do unconsciously that which they have not yet learned to do consciously—namely, to concentrate the mind periodically on the inward silence, and meditate, though very briefly, on high and holy things. The man who has not learned to control and purify his mind in seasons of chosen solitude, yet whose awakening aspirations grope for something higher and nobler than he yet possesses, feels the necessity for the aid of ceremonial religion; but he who has taken himself in hand with a view to self-conquest, who withdraws into solitude in order to grapple with his lower nature, and masterfully bend his mind in holy directions, requires no further aid from book or priest or Church. The Church does not exist for the pleasure of the saint but for the elevation of the sinner.

In solitude a man gathers strength to meet the difficulties and temptations of life, knowledge to understand and conquer them, and wisdom to transcend them. As a building is preserved and sustained by virtue of the foundation which is hidden and unobserved, so a man is maintained perpetually in strength and peace by virtue of his lonely hour of intense thought which no eye beholds.

It is in solitude only that a man can be truly revealed to himself, that he can come to understand his real nature, with all its powers and possibilities. The voice of the spirit is not heard in the hubbub of the world and amid the clamours of conflicting desires. There can be no spiritual growth without solitude.

There are those who shrink from too close a scrutiny of themselves, who dread too complete a self-revelation, and who fear that solitude which would leave them alone with their own thoughts and call up before their mental vision the wraith of their desires. And so they go where the din of pleasure is loudest and where the reproving voice of Truth is drowned. But he who loves Truth, who desires and seeks wisdom, will be much alone. He will seek the fullest, clearest revelation of himself, will avoid the haunts of frivolity and noise, and will go where the sweet, tender voice of the spirit of Truth can speak within him and be heard.

Men go after much company and seek out new excitements, but they are not acquainted with peace; in diverse paths of pleasure they search for happiness but they do not come to rest; through diverse ways of laughter and feverish delirium they wander after gladness and life, but their tears are many and grievous, and they do not escape death.

Drifting upon the ocean of life in search of selfish indulgences men are caught in its storms and only after many tempests and much privation do they fly to the Rock of Refuge which rests in the deep silence of their own being.

While a man is absorbed in outward activities he is giving out his energies and is becoming spiritually weaker, and in order to retain his moral vigour he must resort to solitary meditation. So needful is this that he who neglects it loses or does not attain the right knowledge of life; nor does he comprehend and overcome those most deeply rooted and subtlest of sins which appear like virtues deceiving the elect, and to which all but the truly wise succumb.

"True dignity abides with him alone,
Who, in the silent hour of inward thought,

Can still suspect and still revere himself
In lowliness of heart."

He who lives, without ceasing in outward excitement lives most in disappointments and griefs. Where the sounds of pleasure are greatest heart-emptiness is the keenest and deepest. He, also, whose whole life, even if not one of lust for pleasure, is centered in outward works, who deals only with the changing panorama of visible things, never falling back, in solitude, upon the inner and invisible world of permanent being, such a man does not attain knowledge and wisdom, but remains empty; he cannot aid the world, cannot feed its aspirations, for he has no food to offer it, his spiritual store being empty. But he who courts solitude in order to search for the truth of things, who subdues his senses and makes quite his desires, such a man is daily attaining knowledge and wisdom; he becomes filled with the spirit of truth; he can aid the world, for his spiritual store is full, and is kept well replenished.

While a man is absorbed in the contemplation of inward realities he is receiving knowledge and power; he opens himself, like a flower, to the universal light of Truth, and receives and drinks in its life-imparting rays; he also goes to the eternal foundation of knowledge and quenches his thirst in its inspiring waters. Such a man gains, in one hour of concentrated thought, more essential knowledge than a whole year's reading could impart. Being is infinite and knowledge is illimitable and its source inexhaustible, and he who draws upon the innermost depths of his being drinks from the spring of divine wisdom which can never run dry, and quaffs the waters of immortality.

"In man's self arise August anticipations; symbols, types of a dim splendour ever on before In that eternal circle life pursues."

St.Paul, the cruel persecutor and blind bogot, after spending three years alone in the desert, comes forth a loving apostle and an inspired seer. Gautama Siddhartha, the man of the world, after six years (in the forest) of lonely struggle with his passions and intense meditation upon the deep mysteries of his nature, becomes Buddha, the enlightened one, the embodiment of calm, serene wisdom, to whom a heart-thirsty world turns to refreshing waters of immortality. Lao-tze, an ordinary citizen filling a worldly office, in his search for knowledge courts solitude, and discovers Tao, the Supreme Reason, by virtue of which he becomes a world-teacher. Jesus, the unlettered carpenter, after many years of solitary communion upon the mountains with the Unfailing Love and Wisdom, comes forth a blessed saviour of mankind.

Even after they had attained, and had scaled the lofty heights of divine knowledge these Great Souls were much alone, and retired frequently for brief seasons of solitude. The greatest man will fall from his moral height and lose his influence if he neglects that renewal of power which can only be obtained in solitude. These Masters attained their power by consciously harmonising their thoughts and lives with the creative energies within themselves, and by transcending individuality and sinking their petty personal will in the Universal Will they became Masters of Creative Thought, and stand as the loftiest instruments for the outworking of cosmic evolution.

And this is not miraculous, it is a matter of law; it is not mysterious except in so far as law is mysterious. Every man becomes a creative master in so far as he subordinate himself to the universally good and true. Every poet, painter, saint, and sage is the mouth-piece of the Eternal. The perfection of the message varies with the measure of individual selflessness. In so far as self-intervenes the distinctness of the work and message becomes blurred. Perfect selflessness is the acme of genius, the consummation of power.

Such self-abnegation can only be begun, pursued, and completed in solitude. A man cannot gather together and concentrate his spiritual forces while he is en74 gaged in spending those forces in worldly activities, and although after power is attained the balance of forces can be maintained under all circumstances, even in the midst of the antagonistic throng, such power is only secured after many years of frequent and habitual solitude.

Man's true Home is in the Great Silence—this is the source of all that is real and abiding within him; his present nature, however, is dual, and outer activities are necessary. Neither entire solitude nor entire action is the true life in the world, but that is the true life which gathers, in solitude, strength and wisdom to rightly perform the activities of life; and as a man returns to his home in the evening, weary with labour, for that sweet rest and refreshment which will prepare him for another day's toil, so must he would not break down in the labour of life come away form the noise and toil of the world's great workshop and rest for brief periods in his abiding Home in the Silence. He who does this, spending some portion of each day in sacred and purposeful solitude, will become strong and useful and blessed.

Solitude is for the strong, or for those who are ready to become strong. When a man is becoming great, he becomes solitary. He goes in solitude to seek, and that which he seeks, he finds, for there is a Way to all knowledge, all wisdom, all truth, all power. And the Way is forever open, but it lies through soundless solitudes and the unexplored silences of man's being.

17

THE SURVIVAL OF THE FITTEST AS A DIVINE LAW

Nature and Spirit were at one time universally considered to be at enmity, and even to-day the majority of people regard them as opposed to each other; but a fuller knowledge of the Cosmos reveals the sublime fact that the natural and the spiritual are two aspects of One Eternal Truth.

Nature is the Spirit made visible and tangible. The seen is the expressed form and letter of the unseen. We search in trackless deserts of speculation to find the Real, while all the time it stands before us. The return from those weary and fruitless wanderings to Truth is a coming back to the simple and obvious; but whereas we went out with sealed eyes, we come back with them unsealed; we look upon Nature with a vision clarified from ignorance and egotism, and lo! the unclean has become clean, the mortal has become immortal, the natural is seen to be also the spiritual. Thus, when the physical scientist reveals a natural law, he, at the same time, makes known to the understanding mind—whether he himself knows it or not—a spiritual law. The whole universe is spiritual, and every physical law is the letter of a moral principle. When the moral nature of the Cosmos is apprehended, all controversies about matter and spirit—as things opposed—are at an end, and the assiduous worker in physical realms—often spoken of contemptuously as a "materialist"—is seen to be a revealer, as well as the worker in spiritual realms, the two phases of the universe being, as we have pointed out, but two arcs of one perfect whole.

When Charles Darwin made known the law of "the survival of the fittest," he revealed the working of Divine Justice in Nature. The almost universal prejudice and passionate opposition among religious people which the announcement of his discovery aroused was based, not on the fact itself, but upon a total misunderstanding of that law. That opposition has to-day nearly died out; but even yet one frequently hears this law referred to as a "cruel law", and the belief in it denounced as tending to destroy pity and love.

Such people always think of this law as "the survival of the cruelest," or "the survival of the strongest," and here is where the misunderstanding arises. The correct term, "The Survival of the Fittest," must not be lost sight of; for the fittest are never the cruelest, and rarely the strongest. The strongest and curliest creatures have long since passed away, and have given place to weaker, but more intelligent, creatures and beings. Think of the numberless insects, and of the many powerful enemies which beset them on every hand. Yet these wonderful and beautiful creatures continue to flourish, and they owe their continuance to their intelligence, which is greater, better and more fitted to survive than the strength and cruelty of their enemies. For what is the survival of the fittest but the survival of the best? In a world of continual progress it must needs be that the best of every period takes precedence of the worst—the good of the bad, the fit of the unfit. This, indeed, is the very meaning of progress. When we think of progress, we at once think of something, by its superiority—its greater fitness to the time and occasion—taking precedence of something which is inferior and has fallen out of the line of advancement; and this progress, this advancement, this survival of the fittest, resolves itself into a moral principle, into a Divine Law.

Opponents of this teaching tacitly assume that the most selfish are the fittest to survive, and they thereupon condemn the teaching as callous, and accuse Darwin of making selfishness supreme. But the error is theirs, and not Darwin's or the law's. In their prejudice they wrest his meaning to a false issue, and attack that. Their error consists in assuming that the fittest to survive are the most selfish; whereas such are the worst specimens, and not the best. When we realize that the unselfish are more fitted to survive than the selfish, this law assumes an aspect the very opposite from that which its opponents have given it, and we at once see that in it are involved the profoundest moral principles, namely, the principles of Justice and Love.

Remembering that it is the fittest that survive, what, then-in this universe of law and order–constitutes the fittest? It is evident that the fittest are the most advanced specimens of any given species. Not the strongest, not the cruelest, not the most selfish, not even the finest physically; but the most advanced, those most in line with the order of evolution

The fittest at one period are not the fittest at another. There was a time when brute force was dominant; but that was when nothing higher had been evolved. Yet even in that long distant period–ten million years back, when gigantic monsters held sway upon the earthy–something higher was being evolved. Already intelligence, yea, and unselfish love, were beginning to make themselves felt, for those great beasts loved and protected their young; and so all who most unselfishly shield their offspring, be they beasts or men, will be most protected while, obviously, any species that neglected its offspring would rapidly perish. Thus, long, long ages ago, the fragile babe of intelligence was born in the manager of brute force, and since then, through all the ages of struggle, it has been gradually but surely overcoming the brutal strength and terror; so that to-day intelligence has conquered, or almost conquered, for the strongest brutes have passed away forever, having given place to beings physically weaker and smaller, but better, and more morally perfect.

The beginnings of the Divine Love are already in the world. We see its wonderful operation in the few men in who0m it has been perfected, namely, the Great Spiritual Teachers who, by their precepts and the example of their lives, rule the world to-day; and selfish men worship them as God. We see in these men the prophecy of what Love will do in the distant future, when a large number of men possess it in an advanced degree; how selfishness and selfish men will submit to it and be governed by it, as the brutes now submit to man's intelligence and are ruled by it. And this Love is making its appearance not only in the Great Teachers, but in men less evolved; and though in these it is, as yet, in a more or less rudimentary form, nevertheless the stirrings of its gentleness and joy are being felt in many human hearts.

A common argument against the survival of the fittest is that were men to put it into practice they would kill off all their weakling and invalids, preserving only the strong, and Thus, destroying all pity and love and humanity. This argument is a demonstration of the error to which we have already referred. It is ludicrously self-contradictory, for, while it admits that the best elements are pity and love and humanity, it asserts that these would perish if the fittest, or best survived. And here we are at the heart of the whole matter. The best does survive, and, therefore, pity, compassion, and love cannot be overthrown by selfishness is forevery annihilated.

Speaking of human beings, it is plain that the fittest to survive are not the selfish and the cruel, but those who have developed the finest characteristics of kindness, compassion, justice, and love—in a word, the most moral, the purest, and wisest.

To talk about putting this law "into practice" shows ignorance of its nature; for it is independent in its operation, and is always in activity, and all men and creatures obey it; and should ever a race of men, under them is taken notion that they were practicing it, do it such violence as to "kill off their weaklings and invalids," the law would not cease to operate in their case, and they, by virtue of that very law, would soon exterminate themselves.

With the ceaseless march of human progress, cruelty is becoming less and less fitted to survive against the growing intelligence and gentleness. The cruel races have nearly all died out, only disorganized remnants of them remaining. The fierce animals of prey are becoming fewer, and brutal men are now regarded as a menace to society. Gradually and inevitably, also, selfish and aggressive men will come to have less and less power in the world, will become more out of harmony with the growing environment of peace and goodwill, till at last they will pass away from the earth altogether, as the gigantic brutes have passed away, no longer fitted to survive in a world conquered by Love, in which righteousness and truth become triumphant.

Thus, this law, as represented by Darwin, is the aspect, in Nature, of the operation of Justice, or Love; for in the Light of Truth, Justice and Love are seen to be one. The spiritual aspect of the law was intimately known by all the Great Teachers, and men have overlooked the fact that these Teachers embodied it in their teaching. Thus, the precept of Jesus, "The meek shall inherit the earth," is none other than a simple but Divine statement of the survival of the fittest.

18

GREATNESS AND GOODNESS

Goodness, simplicity, greatness—these three are one, and this trinity of perfection cannot be separated. All greatness springs from goodness, and all goodness is profoundly simple, Without goodness there is no greatness. Some men pass through the world as destructive forces, like the tornado or the avalanche, but they are not great; they are to greatness as the avalanche is to the mountain. The work of greatness is enduring and preservative, and not violent and destructive. The greatest souls are the gentlest.

Greatness is never obtrusive. It works in silence, seeking no recognition. This is why it is not easily perceived and recognized. Like the mountain, it towers up in its vastness, so that those in its immediate vicinity, who receive its shelter and shade, do not see it. Its sublime grandeur is only beheld as they recede from it. The great man is not seen by his contemporaries; the majesty of his form is only outlined by its recession in time. This is the awe and enchantment of distance. Men occupy themselves with the small things; their houses, trees, lands. Few contemplate the mountain at whose base they live, and fewer still essay to explore it. But in the distance these small thing disappear, and then the solitary beauty of the mountain is perceived. Popularity, noisy obtrusiveness, and shallow show, these superficialities rapidly disappear, and leave behind no enduring mark: whereas greatness slowly emerges from obscurity, and endures forever.

Jewish Rabbi and rabble alike saw not the divine beauty of Jesus; they saw only an unlettered carpenter. To his acquaintances, Homer was only a blind beggar, but the centuries reveal him as Homer the immortal poet. Two hundred years after the farmer of Stratford (and all that is known of him) has disappeared, the *real* Shakespeare is discerned. All true genius is impersonal. It belongs not to the man through whom it is manifested; it belongs to all. It is a diffusion of pure Truth: the Light of Heaven descending on all mankind.

Every work of genius, in whatsoever department of art, is a symbolic manifestation of impersonal Truth. It is universal, and finds a response in every heart in every age and race. Anything short of this is not genius, is not greatness. That work which defends *a* religion perishes; it is *religion* that lives. Theories about immortality fade away; immortal man endures; commentaries upon Truth come to the dust; Truth alone remains. That only is true in art which represents the True; that only is great in life which is universally and eternally true. And the True is the Good; the Good is the True.

Every immortal work springs from the Eternal Goodness in the human heart, and it is clothed with the sweet and unaffected simplicity of goodness. The greatest art is, like nature, *artless*. It knows no trick, no pose, no studied effort. There are no stage-tricks in Shakespeare; and he is the greatest of dramatists because he is the *simplest*. The critics, not understanding the wise simplicity of greatness, always condemn the loftiest work. They cannot discriminate between the *childish* and the *childlike*. The True, the Beautiful, the Great, is always childlike, and is perennially fresh and young.

The great man is always the good man; he is always simple. He draws from, nay, lives in, the inexhaustible fountain of divine

Goodness within; he inhabits the Heavenly Places; communes with the vanished great ones; lives with the Invisible: he is inspired, and breathes the airs of Heaven.

He who would be great let him learn to be good. He will therefore become great by not seeking greatness. Aiming at greatness a man arrives at nothingness; aiming at nothingness he arrives at greatness. The desire to be great is an indication of littleness, of personal vanity and obtrusiveness. The willingness to disappear from gaze, the utter absence of self-aggrandizement is the witness of greatness.

Littleness seeks and loves authority. Greatness is never authoritative, and it thereby becomes the authority to which the after ages appeal. He who seeks, loses; he who is willing to lose, wins all men. Be thy simple self, thy better self, thy impersonal self, and lo! thou art great! He who selfishly seeks authority shall succeed only in becoming a trembling apologist courting protection behind the back of acknowledged greatness. He who will become the servant of all men, desiring no personal authority, shall live as a man, and shall be called *great*. "Abide in the simple and noble regions of thy life, obey thy heart, and thou shalt reproduce the foreworld again." Forget thine own little self, and fall back upon the Universal self, and thou shalt reproduce, in living and enduring forms, a thousand beautiful experiences; thou shalt find within thyself that simple goodness which is greatness.

"It is as easy to be great as to be small," says Emerson; and he utters a profound truth. Forgetfulness of self is the whole of greatness, as it is the whole of goodness and happiness. In a fleeting moment of self-forgetfulness the smallest soul becomes great; extend that moment indefinitely, and there is a great soul, a great life. Cast away thy personality (thy petty cravings, vanities, and ambitions) as a worthless garment, and dwell in the loving, compassionate, selfless regions of thy soul, and thou art no longer small—thou art great.

Claiming personal authority, a man descends into littleness; practising goodness, a man ascends into greatness. The presumptuousness of the small may, for a time, obscure the humility of the great, but it is at last swallowed up by it, as the noisy river is lost in the calm ocean.

The vulgarity of ignorance and the pride of learning must disappear. Their worthlessness is equal. They have no part in the Soul of Goodness. If thou wouldst do, thou must *be*. Thou shalt not mistake information for Knowledge; thou must know thyself as pure Knowledge. Thou shalt not confuse learning with Wisdom; thou must apprehend thyself as undefiled Wisdom.

Wouldst thou write a living book? Thou must first *live*; thou shalt draw around thee the mystic garment of a manifold experience, and shalt learn, in enjoyment and suffering, gladness and sorrow, conquest and defeat, that which no book and no teacher can teach thee. Thou shalt learn of life, of thy soul; thou shalt tread the Lonely Road, and shalt *become*; thou shalt *be*. Thou shalt then write thy book, and it shall live; it shall be more than a book. Let thy book first live in thee, then shalt thou live in thy book.

Wouldst thou carve a statue that shall captivate the ages, or paint a picture that shall endure? Thou shalt acquaint thyself with the divine Beauty within thee. Thou shalt comprehend and adore the Invisible Beauty; thou shalt know the Principles which are the soul of Form; thou shalt perceive the matchless symmetry and faultless proportions of Life, of Being, of the Universe; Thus, knowing the eternally True thou shalt carve or paint the indescribably Beautiful.

Wouldst thou produce an imperishable poem? Thou shalt

first live thy poem; thou shalt think and act rhythmically; thou shalt find the never-failing source of inspiration in the loving places of thy heart. Then shall immortal lines flow from thee without effort, and. as the flowers of wood and field spontaneously spring, so shall beautiful thoughts grow up in thine heart and, enshrined in words as moulds to their beauty, shall subdue the hearts of men.

Wouldst thou compose such music as shall gladden and uplift the world? Thou shalt adjust thy soul to the Heavenly Harmonies. Thou shalt know that thyself, that life and the universe is Music. Thou shalt touch the chords of Life. Thou shalt know that Music is everywhere; that it is the Heart of Being; then shalt thou hear with thy spiritual ear the Deathless Symphonies.

Wouldst thou preach the living word? Thou shalt forego thyself, and become that Word. Thou shalt know one thing—*that the human heart is good, is divine;* thou shalt live on one thing—*Love*. Thou shalt love all, seeing no evil, thinking no evil, believing no evil; then, though thou speak but little, thy every act shall be a power, thy every word a precept. By thy pure thought, thy selfless deed, though it appear hidden, thou shalt preach, down the ages, to untold multitudes of aspiring souls.

To him who chooses Goodness, sacrificing all, is given that which is more than and includes all. He becomes the possessor of the Best, communes with the Highest, and enters the company of the Great.

The greatness that is flawless, rounded, and complete is above and beyond all art. It is Perfect Goodness in manifestation; therefore the greatest souls are always Teachers.

19

SYMPATHY

"When thy gaze
Turns it on thine own soul, be most severe:
But when it falls upon a fellow-man
Let kindliness control it; and refrain
From that belittling censure that springs forth
From common lips like weeds from marshy soil."

—Ella Wheeler Wilcox

"I do not ask the wounded person how he feels,
I myself become the wounded person."

—Walt Whitman

We can only sympathise with others in so far as we have conquered ourselves. We cannot think and feel for others while we are engaged in condoling with and pitying ourselves; cannot deal tenderly and lovingly with others while we are anxious for our own pre-eminence or for the exclusive preservation of ourselves, our opinions, and our own generally. What is sympathy but thoughtfulness for others in the forgetfulness of self?

To sympathise with others we must first understand them, and to understand them we must put away all personal preconceptions concerning them, and must see them as they are. We must enter into their inner state and become one with them, looking through their mental eyes and comprehending the range of their experience. You cannot, of course, do this with a being whose wisdom and experience are greater than your own; nor can you do it with any if you regard yourself as being on a higher plane than others (for egotism and sympathy cannot dwell together), but you can practise it with all those who are involved in sins and sufferings from which you have successfully extricated yourself, and, though your sympathy cannot embrace and overshadow the man whose greatness is beyond you, yet you can place yourself in such an attitude towards him as to receive the protection of his larger sympathy and so make for yourself an easier way out of the sins and sufferings by which you are still enchained.

Prejudice and ill-will are complete barriers to the giving of sympathy, while pride and vanity are total barriers to its reception. You cannot sympathise with a person for whom you have conceived a hatred; you cannot enjoy the sympathy of one whom you envy. You cannot understand the person whom you dislike, or he for whom, through animal impulse, you have framed an ill-formed affection. You do not, cannot, see him as he is, but see only your own imperfect notions of him; see only a distorted image of him through the exaggerating medium of your illgrounded opinions.

To see others as they are you must not allow impulsive likes and dislikes, powerful prejudices, or egotistic considerations to come between you and them. You must not resent their actions or condemn their beliefs and opinions. You must leave yourself entirely out, and must, for the time being, assume their position. Only in this way can you become en rapport with them, and so fathom their life, their experience, and understand it, and when a man is understood it becomes impossible to condemn him. Men misjudge, condemn, and avoid each other because they do not understand each other, and they do not understand each other because they have not overcome and purified themselves.

Life is growth, development, evolution, and there is no essential distinction between the sinner and the saint—there is only a difference in degree. The saint was once a sinner; the sinner will one day be a saint. The sinner is the child; the saint is the grown man. He who separates himself from sinners, regarding them as wicked men to be avoided, is like a man avoiding contact with little children because they are unwise, disobedient, and play with toys.

All life is one, but it has a variety of manifestations. The grown flower is not something distinct from the tree: it is a part of it; is only another form of leaf. Steam is not something apart from water: it is but another form of water. And in like manner good is transmuted evil: the saint is the sinner developed and transformed.

The sinner is one whose understanding is undeveloped, and he ignorantly chooses wrong modes of action. The saint is one whose understanding is ripened, and he wisely chooses right modes of action. The sinner condemns the sinner, condemnation being a wrong mode of action. The saint never condemns the sinner, remembering that he himself formerly occupied the same place, but thinks of him with deep sympathy, regarding him in the light of a younger brother or a friend, for sympathy is a right and enlightened mode of action.

The perfected saint, who gives synpathy to all, needs it of none, for he has transcended sin and suffering, and lives in the enjoyment of lasting bliss; but all who suffer need sympathy, and all who sin must suffer. When a man comes to under38 stand that every sin, whether of thought or deed, receives its just quota of suffering he ceases to condemn and begins to sympathise, seeing the sufferings which sin entails; and he comes to such understanding by purifying himself.

As a man purges himself of passions, as he transmutes his selfish desires and puts under foot his egotistic tendencies, he sounds the depths of all human experiences—all sins and sufferings and sorrows, all motives and thoughts and deeds—and comprehends the moral law in its perfection. Complete self-conquest is perfect knowledge, perfect sympathy, and he who views men with the stainless vision of a pure heart views them with a pitying heart, sees them as a part of himself, not as something defiled and separate and distinct, but as his very self, sinning as he has sinned, suffering as he has suffered, sorrowing as he has sorrowed, yet, withal, glad in the knowledge that they will come, as he has come, to perfect peace at last.

The truly good and wise man cannot be a passionate partisan, but extends his sympathy to all, seeing no evil in others to be condemned and resisted, but seeing the sin which is pleasant to the sinner, and the after-sorrow and pain which the sinner does not see, and, when it overtakes him, does not understand.

A man's sympathy extends just so far as his wisdom reaches, and no further; and a man only grows wiser as he grows tenderer and more compassionate. To narrow one's sympathy is to narrow one's heart, and so to darken and embitter one's life. To extend and broaden one's sympathy is to enlighten and gladden one's life and to make plainer to others the way of light and gladness.

To sympathise with another is to receive his being into our own, to become one with him, for unselfish love indissolubly unites, and he whose sympathy reaches out to and embraces all humankind and all living creatures has realised his identity and oneness with all, and comprehends the universal Love and Law and Wisdom. Man is shut out from Heaven and Peace and Truth only in so far as he shuts out others from his sympathy. Where his sympathy ends his darkness and torment and turmolis begin, for to shut others out from our love is to shut ourselves out from the blessedness of love, and to become cramped in the dark prison of self.

> "Whoever walks a furlong without sympathy walks to his own funeral dressed in a shroud."

Only when one's sympathy is unlimited is the Eternal Light of Truth revealed; only in the Love that knows no restriction is the boundness bliss enjoyed.

Sympathy is bliss; in it is revealed the highest, purest blessedness. It is divine, for in its reciprocal light all thought of self is lost, and there remains only the pure joy of oneness with others, the ineffable communion of spiritual identity. Where a man ceases to sympathise he ceases to live, ceases to see and realise and know.

One cannot truly sympathise with others until all selfish considerations concerning them are put away, and he who does this and strives to see others as they are, strives to realise their particular sins, temptations, and sorrows, their beliefs, opinions, and prejudices, comes at last to see exactly where they stand in their spiritual evolution, comprehends the arc of their experience, and knows that they cannot for the present act otherwise than they do. He sees that their thoughts and acts are prompted by the extent of their knowledge, or their lack of knowledge, and that if they act blindly and foolishly it is because their knowledge and experience are immature, and they can only come to act more wisely by gradual growth into more enlightened states of mind. He also sees that though this growth can be encouraged, helped, and stimulated by the influence of a riper example, by seasonable words and well-timed instruction, it cannot be unnaturally forced; the flowers of love and wisdom must have time to grow, and the barren branches of hatred and folly cannot be all cut away at once.

Such a man finds the doorway into the inner world of those with whom he comes in contact, and he opens it and enters in and dwells with them in the hidden and sacred sanctuary of their being. And he finds nothing to hate, nothing to revile, nothing to condemn in that sacred place, but something to love and tend, and, in his own heart, room only for greater pity, greater patience, greater love.

He sees that he is one with them, that they are but another aspect of himself, that their natures are not different from his own, except in modification and degree, but are identical with it. If they are acting out certain sinful tendencies he has but to look within to find the same tendencies in himself, albeit, perhaps, restrained or purified; if they are manifesting certain holy and divine qualities he finds the same pure spirit within himself, though, perhaps, in a lesser degree of power and development.

"One touch of nature makes the whole world kin."

The sin of one is the sin of all; the virtue of one is the virtue of all. No man can be separate from another. There is no difference of nature but only difference of condition. If a man thinks he is separated from another by virtue of his superior holiness he is not so separated, and his darkness and delusion are very great. Humanity is one, and in the holy sanctuary of sympathy saint and sinner meet and unite.

It is said of Jesus that He took upon Himself the sins of the whole world—that is, He identified Himself with those sins, and did not regard Himself as essentially separate from sinners but as being of a like nature with them—and his realisation of His oneness with all men was manifested in His life as profound sympathy with those who, for their deep sins, were avoided and cast off by others.

And who is it that is in the greatest need of sympathy? Not the saint, not the enlightened seer, not the perfect man. It is the sinner, the unenlightened man, the imperfect one; and the greater the sin the greater is the need. "I came not to call the righteous but sinners to repentance" is the statement of One who comprehended all human needs. The righteous man does not need your sympathy, but the unrighteous; he who, by his wrong-doing, is laying up for himself long periods of suffering and woe is in need of it.

The flagrantly unrighteous man is condemned, despised, and avoided by those who are living in a similar condition to himself, though for the time being, they may not be subject to his particular form of sin, for that withholding of sympathy and that mutual condemnation which are so rife is the commonest manifestation of that lack of understanding in which all sin takes its rise. While a man is involved in sin he will condemn others who are likewise involved, and the deeper and greater his sin the more severe will be his condemnation of others. It is only when a man begins to sorrow for his sin, and so to rise above it into the clearer light of purity and understanding, that he ceases from condemning others and learns to sympathise with them. But this ceaseless condemnation of each other by those who are involved in the fierce play of the passions must needs, be, for it one of the modes of operation of the Great

Law which universally and eternally obtains, and the unrighteous one who falls under the condemnation of his fellows will the more rapidly reach a higher and nobler condition of heart and life if he humbly accepts the censure of others as the effect of his own sin, and resolves henceforward to refrain from all condemnation of others.

One aspect of sympathy is that of pity—pity for the distressed or pain-stricken, with a desire to alleviate or help them bear their sufferings. The world needs more of this divine quality.

> "For pity makes the world
> Soft to the weak, and noble for the strong."

But it can only be developed by eradicating all hardness and unkindness, all accusation and resentment. He who, when he sees another suffering for his sin, hardens his heart and thinks or says: "It serves him right"-such a one cannot exercise pity nor apply its healing balm. Every time a man acts cruelly towards another (be it only a dumb creature), or refuses to bestow needed sympathy, he dwarfs himself, deprives himself of ineffable blessedness, and prepares himsrelf for suffering.

Another form of sympathy is that of rejoicing with those who are more successful than ourselves, as though their success were our own. Blessed indeed is he who is free from all envy and malice, and can rejoice and be glad when he hears of the good fortune of those who regard him as an enemy.

The protecting of creatures weaker and more indefensible than oneself is another form in which this divine sympathy is manifested. The helpless frailty of the dumb creation calls for the exercise of the deepest sympathy. The glory of superior strength resides in its power to shield, not to destroy. Not by the callous of destruction of weaker things is life truly lived, but by their preservation:

"All life
Is linked and kin,"

and the lowest creature is not separated from the highest but by greater weakness, by lesser intelligence. When we pity and protect we reveal and enlarge the divine life and joy within ourselves. When we thoughtlessly or callously inflict suffering or destroy, then our divine life becomes obscured, and its joy fades and dies. Bodies may feed bodies, and passions passions, but man's divine nature is only nurtured, sustained, and developed by kindness, love, sympathy, and all pure and unselfish acts.

By bestowing sympathy on others we increase our own. Sympathy given can never be wasted. Even the meanest creature will respond to its heavenly touch, for it is the universal language which all creatures understand. I have recently heard a true story of a Dartmoor convict whose terms of incarceration in various convict stations extended to over forty years. As a criminal he was considered one of the most callous and hopelessly abandoned, and the warders found him almost intractable. But one day he caught a mouse—a weak, terrified, hunted thing like himself—and its helpless frality, and the similarity of its condition with his own, appealed to him, and started into flame the divine spark of sympathy which smouldered in his crime-hardened heart, and which no human touch had ever wakened into life.

He kept the mouse in an old boot in his cell, fed, tended, and loved it, and in his love for the weak and helpless he forgot and lost his hatred for the strong. His heart and his hand were no longer against his fellows. He became tractable and obedient to the uttermost. The warders could not understand his change;

it seemed to them little short of miraculous that this most hardened of all criminals should suddenly be transformed into the likeness of a gentle, obedient child. Even the expression of his featires altered remarkably: a pleasing smile began to play around the mouth which had formerly been moved to nothing better than a cruel grin, and the implacable hardness of his eyes disappeared and gave place to a soft, deep, mellow light. The criminal was a criminal no longer; he was saved, converted; clothed, and in his right mind; restored to humaneness and to humanity, and set firmly on the pathway to divinity by pitying and caring for a defenceless creature. All this was made known to the warders shortly afterwards, when, on his discharge, he took the mouse away with him.

Thus, sympathy bestowed increases its store in our own hearts, and enriches and fructifies our own life. Sympathy given is blessedness received; sympathy withheld is blessedness forfeited. In the measure that a man increases and enlarges his sympathy so much nearer does he approach the ideal life, the perfect blessedness; and when his heart has become so mellowed that no hard, bitter, or cruel thought can enter and detract from its permanent sweetness, then indeed is he richly and divinely blessed.

20

FIRST STEPS IN THE HIGHER LIFE

Seeing that the Path of Virtue is the Path of Knowledge, and that before the all-embracing Principles of Truth can be comprehended, perfection in the more lowly steps must be acquired, how, then, shall a disciple of Truth begin?

How shall one who aspires to the righting of his mind and the purification of his heart—that heart which is the fountain and repository of all the issues of life—learn the lessons of Virtue? How does he Thus, build himself up in the strength of knowledge, destroying ignorance and the ills of life? What are the first lessons, the first steps? How are they learned? How are they practiced? How are they mastered and understood?

The first lessons consist in overcoming those wrong mental conditions which are most easily eradicated, and which are the common barriers to spiritual progress, as well as in practicing the simple domestic and social virtues. The reader will be better aided if I group and classify the first ten steps in three lessons as follows: Vices of the Body to be Overcome and Eradicated

(First Lesson: Discipline of the Body)

1st step: Idleness, Laziness or Indolence
2nd step: Self-Indulgence or Gluttony

(Second Lesson: Discipline of Speech)

3rd step: Slander
4th step: Gossip and Idle Conversation
5th step: Abusive and Unkind Speech
6th step: Frivolity or Irreverent Speech
7th step: Critical, Captious or Fault-finding Speech

(Third Lesson: Discipline of Tendencies)

8th step: Unselfish Performance of Duty
9th step: Unswerving Rectitude or Moral Integrity
10th step: Unlimited Forgiveness

The two vices of the body, and the five of the tongue, are so called because they are manifested in the body and tongue. Also, by so definitely classifying them, the mind of the reader will be better helped. But it must be clearly understood that these vices arise primarily in the mind, and are wrong conditions of the heart worked out in the body and the tongue.

The existence of such chaotic conditions is an indication that the mind is altogether unenlightened as to the real meaning and purpose of life, and their eradication is the beginning of a virtuous, steadfast, and enlightened life.

But how shall these vices be overcome and eradicated? By first, and at once, checking and controlling their outward manifestations and by suppressing the wrong act. This will stimulate the mind to watchfulness and reflection until, by repeated practice, it will come to perceive and understand the dark, wrong, and erroneous conditions of mind, out of which such acts spring. It will then abandon them entirely.

It will be seen that the first step in the discipline of the mind is the overcoming of indolence or laziness. This is the easiest step, and until it is perfectly accomplished, the other steps cannot be taken. The clinging to indolence constitutes a complete barrier to the Path of Truth. Indolence consists in giving the body more ease and sleep than it requires, in procrastinating, and in shirking and neglecting those things which should receive immediate attention.

This condition of laziness must be overcome by rousing up the body at an early hour, giving it just the amount of sleep it requires for complete recuperation, and by doing promptly and vigorously, every task, every duty, no matter how small, as it comes along.

On no account should food or drink be taken in bed. And to lie in bed after one has awakened, indulging in ease and reverie, is a habit fatal to promptness and resolution of character, and purity of mind. Nor should one attempt to do his thinking at such a time. Strong, pure, and true thinking is impossible under such circumstances. A man should go to bed to sleep, not to think. He should get up to think and work, not to sleep.

The next step is the overcoming of self-indulgence or gluttony. The glutton is he who eats for animal gratification only, without considering the true end and object of eating. He eats more than his body requires, and is greedy after sweet things and rich dishes.

Such undisciplined desire can only be overcome by reducing the quantity of food eaten, and the number of meals per day, and by resorting to a simple and uninvolved diet. Regular hours should be set apart for meals, and eating at other times should be rigidly avoided. Suppers should be abolished, as they are altogether unnecessary, and promote heavy sleep and cloudiness of mind.

The pursuit of such a method of discipline will rapidly bring the once ungoverned appetite under control, and as the sensual sin of self-indulgence is taken out of the mind, the right selection of foods will be instinctively and infallibly adapted to the purified mental condition.

It should be well borne in mind that a change of heart is the needful thing, and that any change of diet which does not promote this end is futile. When one eats for enjoyment, he is gluttonous. The heart must be purified of sensual craving and gustatory lust.

When the body is well controlled and firmly guided; when that which is to be done is done vigorously; when no task or duty is delayed; when early rising has become a delight; when frugality, simplicity, temperance, and abstinence are firmly established; when one is contented with the food which is put before him, no matter how scanty and plain, and the craving for gustatory pleasure is at an end—then the first two steps in the Higher Life are accomplished. Then is the first great lesson in Truth learned. Thus, is established in the heart the foundation of a poised, self-governed, virtuous life.

The next lesson is the lesson of Virtuous Speech, in which there are five orderly steps. The first of these is overcoming the habit of slanderous speech. Slander consists of inventing or repeating unkind and evil reports about others, in exposing and magnifying the faults of others, or of absent friends, and in introducing unworthy insinuations. The elements of thoughtlessness, cruelty, insincerity, and untruthfulness enter into every slanderous act.

He who aims at the living of the right life will commence to check the cruel word of slander before it has gone forth from his lips. He will then check and eliminate the insincere thought which gave rise to it.

He will watch that he does not vilify or defame anyone.

He will refrain from disparaging, defaming, and condemning the absent friend, whose face he has so recently smiled into or kissed, or whose hand he has shaken. He will not say of another that which he dare not say to his face. Thus, coming at last to think sacredly of the character and reputation of others, he will destroy those wrong conditions of mind which give rise to slander.

The next step is the overcoming of gossip and idle conversation. Idle speech consists in talking about the private affairs of others, in talking merely to pass away the time, and in engaging in aimless and irrelevant conversation. Such an ungoverned condition of speech is the outcome of an ill-regulated mind.

The man of virtue will bridle his tongue, and Thus, learn how rightly to govern the mind. He will not let his tongue run idly and foolishly, but will make his speech strong and pure, and will either talk with a purpose or remain silent.

Abusive and unkind speech is the next vice to be overcome. The man who abuses and accuses others has himself wandered far from the Right Way. To hurl hard words and names at others is to sink deeply into folly. When a man is inclined to abuse, curse, and condemn others, let him restrain his tongue and look within himself. The virtuous man refrains from all abusive language and quarreling. He employs only words that are useful, necessary, pure, and true.

The sixth step is the overcoming of levity, or irreverent speech. Light and frivolous talking; the repeating of crude jokes; the telling of vulgar stories, having no other purpose than to raise an empty laugh; offensive familiarity, and the employment of contemptuous and disrespectful words when speaking to or of others, and particularly of one's elders and those who rank as one's teachers, guardians or superiors—all of this will he put away by the lover of Virtue and Truth.

Upon the altar of irreverence absent friends and companions are immolated for the passing excitement of a momentary laugh, and all the sanctity of life is sacrificed to the zest for ridicule. When respect towards others and the giving of reverence where reverence is due are abandoned, Virtue is abandoned. When modesty, significance, and dignity are eliminated from speech and behavior, Truth is lost. Yea, even its entrance gate is hidden away and forgotten.

Irreverence is degrading even in the young, but when it accompanies grey hairs, and appears in the demeanor of the preacher—this is indeed a piteous spectacle. And when this can be imitated and followed after, then are the blind leading the blind, then have elders, preachers, and people lost their way.

The virtuous will be of earnest and reverent speech. He will think and speak of the absent as he thinks and speaks of the dead—tenderly and sacredly. He will put away thoughtlessness, and watch that he does not sacrifice his dignity to gratify a passing impulse to frivolity and superficiality. His humor will be pure and innocent, his voice will be subdued and musical, and his soul will be filled with grace and sweetness as he succeeds in conducting himself as becomes a man of Truth.

The last step in the second lesson is the overcoming of criticism, or fault-finding speech. This vice of the tongue consists in magnifying and harping on small or apparent faults, in foolish quibbling and hair-splitting, and in pursuing vain arguments based upon groundless suppositions, beliefs, and opinions.

Life is short and real, and sin, sorrow and pain are not remedied by carping and contention. The man who is ever on the watch to catch at the words of others in order to contradict and dispute them, has yet to reach the higher way of holiness, the truer life of self-surrender. The man who is ever on the alert to check his own words in order to soften and purify them will find the higher way and the truer life. He will conserve his energies, maintain his composure of mind, and preserve within himself the spirit of Truth.

When the tongue is well controlled and wisely subdued; when selfish impulses and unworthy thoughts no longer rush to the tongue demanding utterance; when the speech has become harmless, pure, gentle, gracious, and purposeful, and no word is uttered but in sincerity and honesty—then are the five steps to virtuous speech accomplished, then is the second great lesson in Truth learned and mastered.

And now some will ask, "But why all this discipline of the body and restraint of the tongue? Surely the Higher Life can be realized and known without such strenuous labor, such incessant effort and watchfulness?" No, it cannot. In the spiritual as the material, nothing is done without labor, and the higher cannot be known until the lower is fulfilled.

Can a man make a table before he has learned how to handle a tool and drive a nail? And can a man fashion his mind in accordance with Truth before he has overcome the slavery of his body?

As the intricate subtleties of language cannot be understood and wielded before the alphabet and the simplest words are mastered, neither can the deep subtleties of the mind be understood and purified before the ABC of right conduct is perfectly acquired.

As for the labor involved—does not the youth joyfully and patiently submit himself to a seven-years' apprenticeship in order to master a craft? And does he not, day by day, carefully and faithfully carry out every detail of his master's instructions, looking forward to the time when, perfected through obedience and practice, he shall be himself a master?

Where is the man who sincerely aims at excellence in music, painting, literature, or in any trade, business, or profession who is not willing to give his whole life to the acquirement of that particular perfection? Shall labor, then, be considered where the very highest excellence is concerned—the excellence of Truth?

He who says, "The Path which you have pointed out is too difficult; I must have Truth without labor, salvation without effort," that man will not find his way out of the confusions and sufferings of selfhood. He will not find the calm, well-fortified mind and the wisely ordered life. His love is for ease and enjoyment, and not for Truth.

He who, deep in his heart, adores Truth, and aspires to know it, will consider no labor too great to be undertaken, but will adopt it joyfully and pursue it patiently. By perseverance in practice he will come to the knowledge of Truth.

The necessity for this preliminary discipline of the body and tongue will be more clearly perceived when it is fully understood that all these wrong outward conditions are merely the expressions of wrong conditions of the heart. An indolent body means an indolent mind; an ill-regulated tongue reveals an ill-regulated mind, and the process of remedying the manifested condition is really a method of rectifying the inward state.

Moreover, the overcoming of these conditions is only a small part of what is really involved in the process. The ceasing from evil leads to, and is inseparably connected with, the practice of good. While a man is overcoming laziness and self-indulgence, he is really cultivating and developing the virtues of abstinence, temperance, punctuality, and self-denial. He is acquiring the strength, energy, and resolve which are indispensable to the successful accomplishment of the higher tasks. While he is overcoming the vices of speech, he is developing the virtues of truthfulness, sincerity, reverence, kindliness, and self-control, and is gaining that mental steadiness and fixedness of purpose, without which the more remote subtleties of the mind cannot be regulated, and the higher stages of conduct and enlightenment cannot be reached.

Also, as he has to do right, his knowledge deepens, and his insight is intensified. Just as a child's heart is glad when a school task is mastered, so with each victory achieved, the man of virtue experiences a bliss which the seeker after pleasure and excitement can never know.

And now we come to the third lesson in the Higher Life, which consists of practicing and mastering, in one's daily life, three great fundamental Virtues:

1) Unselfish Performance of Duty
2) Unswerving Rectitude (Moral Integrity)
3) Unlimited Forgiveness

Having prepared the mind by overcoming the more surface and chaotic conditions mentioned in the first two lessons, the striver after Virtue and Truth is now ready to enter upon greater and more difficult tasks, and to control and purify the deeper motives of the heart.

Without the right performance of duty, the higher virtues cannot be known, and Truth cannot be apprehended. Duty is generally regarded as an irksome labor, a compulsory something which must be toiled through, or be in some way avoided. This way of regarding duty proceeds from a selfish condition of mind, and a wrong understanding of life. All duty should be regarded as sacred, and it s faithful and unselfish performance one of the leading rules of conduct. All personal and selfish considerations should be extracted and cast away from the doing of one's duty, and when this is done, duty ceases to be irksome, and becomes joyful. Duty is only irksome to him who craves some selfish enjoyment or benefit for himself. Let the man who is chafing under the irksomeness of his duty look to himself, and he will find that his wearisomeness proceeds, not from the duty itself, but from his selfish desire to escape it.

He who neglects duty, be it great or small, or of a public or private nature, neglects Virtue. He who in his heart rebels against duty, rebels against Virtue. When Duty becomes a thing of love, and when every particular duty is done accurately, faithfully, and dispassionately, there is much subtle selfishness removed from the heart, and a great step is taken towards the heights of Truth. The virtuous man concentrates his mind on the perfect doing of his own duty, and does not interfere with the duty of another.

The ninth step is the practice of Unswerving Rectitude or Moral Integrity. This Virtue must be firmly established in the mind, and so enter into every detail of a man's life. All dishonesty, deception, trickery, and misrepresentation must be forever put away, and the heart purged of every vestige of insincerity and deception. The least digression from the path of rectitude or righteousness is a deviation from Virtue.

There must be no extravagance and exaggeration of speech, but the simple truth should be stated. Engaging in deception, no matter how apparently insignificant, for boastful pride, or with the hope of personal advantage, is a state of delusion which one should make efforts to dispel. It is demanded of the man of Virtue that he shall not only practice the most rigid honesty in thought, word, and deed, but that he shall be exact in his statements, omitting and adding nothing to the actual truth.

In Thus, shaping his mind to the principle of Rectitude or moral integrity, he will gradually come to deal with people and things in a just and impartial spirit, considering equity before himself, and viewing all things with freedom from personal bias, passion, and prejudice. When the Virtue of Rectitude is fully practiced and comprehended, so that all temptation to untruthfulness and insincerity has ceased, then is the heart made purer and nobler. Then is character strengthened, and knowledge enlarged, and life takes on a new meaning and a new power. Thus, is the ninth step accomplished.

The tenth step is the practice of Unlimited Forgiveness. This consists in overcoming the sense of injury which springs from vanity, selfishness and pride; and in exercising disinterested charity and large-heartedness towards all. Spite, retaliation, and revenge are so utterly ignoble, so base, and so small and foolish, as to be altogether unworthy of being noticed or harbored. No one who fosters such conditions in his heart can lift himself above folly and suffering, and guide his life aright. Only by casting them away, and ceasing to be moved by them, can a man's eyes be opened to the true way of life. Only by developing a forgiving and charitable spirit can he hope to approach and perceive the strength and beauty of a well-ordered life.

In the heart of the strongly virtuous man, no feeling of personal injury can arise. He has put away all retaliation, and has no enemies. If other men should regard themselves as his enemies, he will regard them kindly, understanding their ignorance, and making full allowance for it.

When this state of heart is arrived at, then the tenth step in the discipline of one's selfseeking inclinations is accomplished. Then the third great lesson in Virtue and Knowledge is learned and mastered.

Having Thus, laid down the first ten steps and three lessons in right-doing and rightknowing, I leave those of my readers who are prepared for them to learn and master them in their everyday life.

There is, of course, a still higher discipline of the body, a more far-reaching discipline of the tongue, and greater and more all-embracing virtues to acquire and understand before the highest state of bliss and knowledge can be grasped. But it is not my purpose to deal with them here. I have expounded only the first and easiest lessons on the Higher Path, and by the time these are thoroughly mastered, the reader will have become so purified, strengthened, and enlightened, that he will not be left in the dark as to his future progress.

Those of my readers who have completed these three lessons will already have perceived, beyond and above, the high altitudes of Truth, and the narrow and precipitous track which leads to them, and will choose whether they shall proceed.

The straight Path which I have laid down can be pursued by all with greater profit to themselves and to the world. And even those who do not aspire to the attainment of Truth, will develop greater intellectual and moral strength, finer judgment, and deeper peace of mind by perfecting themselves in this Path. Nor will their material prosperity suffer by this change of heart; nay, it will be rendered truer, purer, and more enduring. For if there is one who is capable of succeeding and fitted to achieve, it is the man who has abandoned the petty weaknesses and everyday vices of his kind, who is strong enough to rule his body and mind, and who pursues with fixed resolve the path of unswerving integrity and sterling virtue.

21

ASPIRATION

With the clear perception of one's own ignorance comes the desire for enlightenment, and Thus, in the heart is born Aspiration, the rapture of the saints.

On the wings of aspiration man rises from earth to heaven, from ignorance to knowledge, from the under darkness to the upper light. Without it he remains a groveling animal, earthly, sensual, unenlightened, and uninspired.

Aspiration is the longing for heavenly things—for righteousness, compassion, purity, love—as distinguished from desire, which is the longing for earthly things—for selfish possessions, personal dominance, low pleasures, and sensual gratifications.

As a bird deprived of its wings cannot soar, so a man without aspiration cannot rise above his surroundings and become master of his animal inclinations. He is the slave of passions, is subject to others, and is carried hither and thither by the changing current of events.

For one to begin to aspire means that he is dissatisfied with his low status, and is aiming at a higher condition. It is a sure sign that he is aroused out of his lethargic sleep of animality, and has become conscious of nobler attainments and a fuller life.

Aspiration makes all things possible. It opens the way to advancement. Even the highest state of perfection conceivable it brings near and makes real and possible; for that which can be conceived can be achieved.

Aspiration is the twin angel to inspiration. It unlocks the gates of joy. Singing accompanies soaring. Music, poetry, prophecy, and all high and holy instruments are at last placed in the hands of those whose aspirations flag not, whose spirit does not fail.

So long as animal conditions taste sweet to a man, he cannot aspire; he is already satisfied. But when their sweetness turns to bitterness, then in his sorrow he thinks of nobler things. When he is deprived of earthly joy, he aspires to the joy which is heavenly. It is when impurity turns to suffering that purity is sought. Truly aspiration rises, phoenix-like, from the dead ashes of repentance, but on its powerful pinions man can reach the heaven of heavens.

The man of aspiration has entered the way which ends in peace, and surely he will reach that end if he neither stays nor turns back. If he constantly renews his mind with glimpses of the heavenly vision, he will reach the heavenly state.

Man attains in the measure that he aspires. His longing to be is the gauge of what he can be. To fix the mind is to foreordain the achievement. As man can experience and know all low things, so he can experience and know all high things. As he has become human, so can he become divine. The turning of the mind in high and divine directions is the sole and needful task.

What is impurity but the impure thoughts of the thinker? What is purity but the pure thoughts of the thinker? One man does not do the thinking of another. Each man is pure or impure of himself alone.

If a man thinks, "It is through others, or circumstances, or heredity that I am impure," how can he hope to overcome his errors? Such a thought will check all holy aspirations and bind him to the slavery of passion.

When a man fully perceives that his errors and impurities are his own, that they are generated and fostered by himself, that he alone is responsible for them, then he will aspire to overcome them. The way of attainment will be opened up to him, and he will see from where and to what destination he is traveling.

The man of passion sees no straight path before him, and behind him is all fog and gloom. He seizes the pleasure of the moment and does not strive for understanding or think of wisdom. His way is confused, turbulent, and troubled, and his heart is far from peace.

The man of aspiration sees before him the pathway up the heavenly heights, and behind him are the circuitous routes of passion up which he has hitherto blindly groped. Striving for understanding, and his mind set on wisdom, his way is clear, and his heart already experiences a foretaste of the final peace.

Men of passion strive mightily to achieve little things—things which speedily perish, and, in the place where they were, leave nothing to be remembered.

Men of aspiration strive with equal might to achieve great things—things of virtue, of knowledge, of wisdom, which do not perish, but stand as monuments of inspiration for the uplifting of humankind.

As the merchant achieves worldly success by persistent exertion, so the saint achieves spiritual success by aspiration and endeavor. One becomes a merchant, the other a saint, by the particular direction in which his mental energy is guided.

When the rapture of aspiration touches the mind, it at once refines it, and the dross of its impurities begins to fall away. While aspiration holds the mind, no impurity can enter it, for the impure and the pure cannot at the same moment occupy the thought. But the effort of aspiration is at first spasmatic and short-lived. The mind falls back into its habitual error, and must be constantly renewed.

The lover of the pure life renews his mind daily with the invigorating glow of aspiration. He rises early, and fortifies his mind with strong thoughts and strenuous endeavor. He knows that the mind is of such a nature that it cannot remain for a moment unoccupied, and that if it is not held and guided by high thoughts and pure aspirations, it will assuredly he enslaved and misguided by low thoughts and base desires.

Aspiration can be fed, fostered, and strengthened by daily habit, just as is desire. It can be sought, and admitted into the mind as a divine guide, or it can be neglected and shut out. To retire for a short time each day to some quiet spot, preferably in the open air, and there call up the energies of the mind in surging waves of holy rapture, is to prepare the mind for great spiritual victories and destinies of divine import. For such a rapture is the preparation for wisdom and the prelude to peace.

Before the mind can contemplate pure things it must be lifted up to them, it must rise above impure things; and aspiration is the instrument by which this is accomplished. By its aid the mind soars swiftly and surely into heavenly places, and begins to experience divine things. It begins to accumulate wisdom, and to learn to guide itself by an ever-increasing measure of the divine light of pure knowledge.

To thirst for righteousness; to hunger for the pure life; to rise in holy rapture on the wings of angelic aspiration—this is the right road to wisdom. This is the right striving for peace. This is the right beginning of the way divine.

22

THE NEW COURAGE

The virtue of courage is generally referred to in its physical manifestation, and it is significant in this particular-that its symbol is a beast of prey, namely, the lion. The dictionary rendering adheres to this physical aspect of courage, for on turning up the word I find its meanings are given as "bravery, fearlessness, intrepidity," no other rendering being given. The solider is the human type of courage, and the current sayings concerning courage are: "As courageous as a lion" and "As brave as a solider."

The lion and the solider are alike fearless in attack and defense, and both will forfeit life rather than yield; but it is an entirely animal physical attack and defense. Courage, however, cannot be confined to this phase—indeed, this is its lowest manifestation—for it has many aspects, many modes of action; and as man rises in the moral and spiritual scale his courage becomes transmuted, taking a newer and higher form. But before proceeding to the highest form of courage, which is the subject of this article, it is necessary that the lower forms should be first considered.

With the physical form of courage already referred to all are familiar. It is common both to animals and men. It arises in fearlessness. Its twofold mode of action is attack and defense. It will be seen, however, that this kind of courage is inevitably associated with suffering, even with destruction and death, as daily manifested both in the animal and human spheres of life; self-protection being its dominant motive, whether in attack or defense.

But man is not only and merely an animal, a physical being; he is also a moral and intellectual being; and along with his moral evolution he began to develop a higher kind of courage-not the highest, or the New Courage herein referred to; but yet a great advance on the purely animal courage, namely, moral courage. In physical courage the other person's body or property is attacked, while one's own body or property is defended. In moral courage the other person's ideas, opinions, or principles are attacked, one's own ideas, opinions, and principles being defended. There is the same fearlessness, the same attack and defense so far as the spirit of courage is concerned; but as regards its letter, these conditions have undergone a change; their physical aspect has disappeared, and, having undergone a process of transmutation, has reappeared in a new form, for moral courage is concerned not with persons as persons, but with their principles. It is, indeed, purely mental; and while it is still concerned with destruction and is associated with suffering, the destruction is a bloodless and intellectual one, namely, the destruction of other men's opinions, and its suffering is mental and not physical.

This form of courage is now generally recognized, and is always referred to as moral courage, to distinguish it from common or physical courage. It is, without doubt, a comparatively recent development in the evolution of the race, and is entirely absent from animals. A few thousand years ago it was, in all probability, an exceeding rare and new faculty, and it is still in process of development, large numbers of the race not yet having evolved it; for while it is probable that at least seventy-five per cent of the race possess a considerable development of physical courage, it is doubtful whether twenty per cent possess any marked degree of moral courage; so much so that those in full possession of it are marked off from their fellows as men of a higher grade of character, and generally-though not necessarily and always—as leaders of men in their particular sphere of action.

But the New Courage, up to a consideration of which the preceding remarks have been leading, is a still higher form of courage-is, indeed, as much above and beyond moral courage as moral courage is above and beyond physical courage; and is as separate and distinct from it as that is from its precedent form. I have called it the New Courage because it is now new in the race, its manifestation being at present very rare, and, therefore, little understood. Though very different from moral courage, it results from it, just as moral courage, though very different from physical courage, though very different from physical courage results from it. Physical courage is of the animal; moral courage is of the human; the New Courage is of the Divine. The new Courage is, therefore, Divine fearlessness as distinguished from animal or human fearlessness.

This Divine fearlessness has a twofold aspect. It at first consists in fearlessly attacking and overcoming the enemies within one's own mind—instead of the enemies without, as in the other two forms of courage—and is afterwards characterized by an entirely new method of conduct towards others, especially where external enmity and opposition have to be met. It is its latter and perfected stage with which we are here concerned—that is, with its outward manifestation.

We have seen how a man having physical courage acts in defense of his life and property; also how a man having moral courage acts in defense of his opinions; and now, how does one act who has Divine courage?

He who has the New Courage does not attack other men or defend himself; does not attack their opinions or defend his own; he is the defender of all men, and that from which he defends them is their own folly, their own ungoverned passions. While never seeking to protect himself, he so acts as to shield others from their deadliest enemy, namely, the evil within themselves.

Both physical and moral courage make much noise. In the one there is the clash of arms and the roar of artillery, along with the shouts of the victories and the groans of the dying; in the other there is the fierce war of opinions and the clamor of conflicting tongues. But in the New Courage there is a profound silence; yet this silence has more influence and enduring power in one man than that noise has in entire humanity. The New Courage may, indeed be described as the courage to be silent. Thus, when the man of Divine courage is attacked, abused, or slandered, he remains serenely silent. Yet this is not a proud and selfish silence. It is a silence based upon a right knowledge of life and having a profound and beneficent purpose; that purpose being the good of the attacking person (and, through him, of all mankind) by protecting him from the evil passion by which he is so injuriously influenced.

To remain silent, calm, and compassionate in the midst of a seething sea of human passions externally pressing upon one-to achieve this requires a lofty courage such as is yet almost unknown to men; so much so that the few men who have it, although misunderstood and persecuted through life, are afterwards worshiped by mankind as Divine and miraculous beings. And here we see how this courage continucs to operate even after its possessor is gone from mortal vision.

The physically courageous man conquers another in fight; the morally courageous man conquers the opinions of many men, and wins thousands to his cause; but the divinely courageous man conquers the world, and his conquest is one of blessedness and peace, and not of bloodshed or party strife.

In the New Courage, attack and defense, and they obtain in the two lower kinds of courage, have entirely disappeared. Nevertheless, they have not been destroyed; they still exist in the sporty, but have become blended into one, have been transmuted into a sublime and universal kindness; for when the Divine man refrains from engaging in combat with his adversary, and lets him go feeling that he has all the victory, it is because his thought is all for his mistaken enemy, and not for his own defense. He is prompted by a profound compassion for his enemy, a compassion based on Divine and perfect knowledge; and if his silent act does not always subdue the passions of his adversary at the time being, it subdues the passions of thousands of men through hundreds of future generations merely by its recital, so great and far-reaching is the power of one deed of truth.

In the New Courage, then, silent kindness (and by this meant something vastly different from that human impulse commonly called kindness) is both attack and defense. Instead of attempting to conquer passion by fiercer passion—which is the human way—it conquers it, and far more successfully, by it's opposite, namely, gentleness, which is the Divine way. In the human sense, passion is not opposed at all, but is left alone; yet, in reality, it is opposed by something far more powerful than passion, for in all combats between Divine gentleness and human passion gentleness is the supreme victor. Thus, the man of Divine courage, while, viewed from the lower standards of bravery, is not protecting or defending himself, and may for the time being be regarded as a coward, is, in reality, defending himself far more perfectly and successfully than the passionate fighters and partisans; for he who protects his enemy with love, and shields all men with the acts of Divine gentleness, is throwing around himself an eternal shield and protection.

When the Buddha was abused and falsely accused by His enemies, He always remained silent; and it not infrequently happened that those who came as accusing enemies went away as worshiping friends and disciples, so powerful was His silent gentleness.

It will be long, as we count time, before such courage becomes general in the race; but everything is making towards it. Other men will come who possess it, and then more an more, until at last the race will stand at this Divine level. Then selfishness and sorrow will be ended, and the painful conflict of human passions will no more be heard upon earth.

23

BURDEN-DROPPING

"This to me is life;
That if life be a burden, I will join
To make it but the burden of a song."

—Bailey

"Have you heard that it was good to gain the day?
I also say it is good to fall, battles are lost in the same spirit in which they are won."

—Walt Whitman

We hear and read much about burden-bearing, but of the better way of burdendropping very little is heard or known. Yet why should you go about with an oppressive weight at your heart when you might relieve yourself of it and move amongst your fellows heart-free and cheerful? No man carries a load upon his back except to necessarily transfer something from one place to another; he does not saddle his shoulders with a perpetual burden, and then regard himself as a martyr for his pains; and why should you impose upon your mind a useless burden, and then add to its weight the miseries of self-condolence and self-pity? Why not abandon both your load and your misery, and Thus, add to the gladness of the world by first making yourself glad? No reason can justify, and no logic support, the ceaseless carrying of a grievous load. As in things material a load is only undertaken as a necessary means of transference, and is never a source of sorrow, so in things spiritual a burden should only be taken up as a means towards some good and necessary end, which, when attained, the burden is put aside; and the carrying of such a burden, far from being a source of grief would be a cause for rejoicing.

We say that bodily mortifications which some religious ascetics inflict upon themselves are unnecessary and vain; and are the mental mortifications which so many people inflict upon themselves less unnecessary and vain?

Where is the burden which should cause unhappiness or sorrow? It does not exist. If a thing is to be done let it be done cheerfully, and not with inward groanings and lamentations. It is of the highest wisdom to embrace necessity as a friend and guide. It is of the greatest folly to scowl upon necessity as an enemy, and to wish or try to overcome or avoid her. We meet our own at every turn, and duties only become oppressive loads when we refuse to recognize and embrace them. He who does any necessary thing in a niggardly and complaining spirit, hunting the while after unnecessary pleasures, lashes himself with the scorpions of misery and disappointment, and imposes upon himself a doubly-weighted burden of weariness and unrest under which he incessantly groans.

"Wake thou, O self, to better things;
To yonder heights uplift thy wings;
Take up the psalm of life anew;
Sing of the good, sing of the true;
Sing of full victory o'er wrong;

Make though a richer, sweeter song;
Out of thy doubting, care and pain
Weave thou a joyous, glad refrain;
Out of thy thorns a crown weave thou
Of rare rejoicing. Sing thou, now."

I will give my cheerful, unselfish, and undivided attention to the doing of all those things which enter into my compact with life, and, though I walk under colossal responsibilities, I shall be unconscious of any troublesome weight or grievous burden.

If it is right and necessary that a thing should be done then the doing of it is good, and it can only become burdensome in wishing not to do it. The selfish wish makes the thing appear evil. If it is neither right nor necesssary that a thing should be done then the doing of it in order to gain some coveted pleasure is folly, which can only lead to burdensome issues.

The duty which you shirk is your reproving angel; the pleasure which you race after is your flattering enemy. Foolish man! when will you turn round and be wise?

It is the beneficence of the universe that it is everywhere, and at all times, urging its creatures to wisdom as it demands coherence of its atoms. That folly and selfishness entail suffering in ever-increasing degrees of intensity is preservative and good, for agony is the enemy of apathy and the herald of wisdom.

What is painful? What is grievous? What is burdensome? Passion is painful; folly is grievous; selfishness is burdensome.

"It is the dark idolatry of self
Which, when our thoughts and actions once are done,
Demands that man should weep, and bleed, and groan."

Eliminate passion, folly and selfishness from your mind and conduct and you will eliminate suffering from your life. Burden-dropping consists in abandoning the inward selfishness and putting pure love in its place. Go to your task with love in your heart and you will go to it light-hearted and cheerful.

The mind, through ignorance creates its own burdens and inflicts its own punishments. No one is doomed to carry any load. Sorrow is not arbitrarily imposed. These things are self-made. Reason is the rightful monarch of the mind, and anarchy reigns in his spiritual kingdom when his throne is usurped by passion. When love of pleasure is to the fore, heaviness and anguish compose the rear. You are free to choose. Even if you are bound by passion, and feel helpless, you have bound yourself, and are not helpless. Where you have bound you can unbind. You have come to your present state by degrees, and you can recover yourself by degrees, can reinstate reason and dethrone passion. The time to avoid evil is before pleasure is embraced, but, once embraced, its train of consequences should teach you wisdom. The time to decide is before responsibilities are adopted, but, once adopted, all selfish considerations, with their attendant grumblings, whinings, and complainings, should be religiously excluded from the heart. Responsibilities lose their weight when carried lovingly and wisely.

What heavy burden is a man weighted with which is not made heavier and more unendurable by weak thoughts of selfish desires? If your circumstances are "trying" it is because you need them and can evolve the strength to meet them. They are trying because there is some weak spot within you, and they will continue to be trying until that spot is eradicated. Be glad that you have the opportunity of becoming stronger and wiser. No circumstances can be trying to wisdom; nothing can weary love. Stop brooding over your own trying circumstances and contemplate the lives of some of those about you.

Here is a woman with a large family who has to make ends meet on a pound a week. She performs all her domestic duties, down to the washing, finds time to attend on sick neighbours, and manages to keep entirely out of the two common quagmires—debt and despondency. She is cheerful from morning to night, and never complains of her "trying circumstances." She is perennially cheerful because she is unselfish. She is happy in the thought that she is the means of happiness to others. Were she to brood upon the holidays, the pretty baubles, the lazy hours of which she is deprived; of the plays she cannot see, the music she cannot hear, the books she cannot read, the parties she cannot attend, the good she might do, the friendships she is debarred from forming; of the many pleasures which might only be hers if her circumstances were more favourable—if she brooded Thus, what a miserable creature she would be! How unbearably labourious her work would become! How every little domestic duty would hang like a millstone about her neck, dragging her down to the grave which, unless she altered her state of mind, she would quickly reach, killed by—selfishness! But, not living in vain desires for herself, she is relieved of all burdens, and is happy. Cheerfulness and unselfishness are sworn friends. Love knows no heavy toil.

Here is another woman, with a private income which is more than sufficient, combined with leisure and luxury, yet, because she is called upon to forfeit a portion of her time, pleasure, and money to discharge some obligation which she wishes to be rid of, and which should be to her a work of loving service, or fostering in her heart some ungratified desire, she is perpetually discontented and unhappy, and complains of "trying circumstances". Discontent and Selfishness are inseparable companions. Self-love knows no joyful labour.

Of the two sets of circumstances above depicted (and life is crowded with such contrasted instances) which are the "trying" conditions? Is it not true that neither of them are trying, and that both are blest or unblest in accordance with the measure of love or selfishness which is infused into them? Is not the root of the whole matter in the mind of the individual and not in the circumstance?

When a man, who has recently taken up the study of some branch of theology, religion, or "occultism," says: "If I had not burdened myself with a wife and family I could have done a great work; and had I known years ago what I know now I would never have married." I know that that man has not yet found the commonest and broadest way of wisdom (for there is no greater folly than regret), and that he is incapable of the great work which he is so ambitious to perform. If a man has such deep love for his fellow-men that he is anxious to do a great work for humanity he will manifest that surpassing love always and in the place where he now is. His home will be filled with it, and the beauty and sweetness and peace of his unselfish love will follow wherever he goes, making happy those about him and transmuting all things into good. The love that goes abroad to air itself, and is undiscoverable at home, is not love—it is vanity.

Have I not seen (Oh, pitiful sight!) the cheerless home and neglected children of the misguided missioner and religionist? It is on such self-delusion as this that self-pity and self-martyrdom ever wait, and its self-inflicted misery is regarded by the deluded one as a holy and religious burden which he or she is called upon to bear.

Only a great man can do a great work; and he will be great

wherever he is, and will do his noble work under whatsoever conditions he may find himself when he has unfolded and revealed that work.

Thou who art so anxious to work for humanity, to help thy fellow-men, begin that work at home; help thyself, thy neighbour, thy wife, thy child. Do not be deluded; until thou doest, with utmost faithfulness, the nearer and the lesser thou canst not do the farther and greater.

If a man has lived many years of his life in lust and selfish pleasure it is in the order of things that his accumulated errors should at last weigh heavily upon him, as, until they are Thus, brought home to him, he will not abandon them, will not exert himself to find a better life; but whilst he regards his self-made, self-imposed burdens as "holy crosses" imposed upon him by the Supreme, or as marks of superior virtue, or as loads which Fate, circumstances, or other people have heaped undeservedly and unjustly upon him, he is but lengthening out his folly, increasing the weight of his burdens, and multiplying his pains and sorrows. Only when such a man wakes up to the truth that his burdens are of his own making, that they are the accumulated effects of his own acts, will he cease from unmanly self-pity and find the better way of burden-dropping; only when he opens his eyes to see that his every thought and act is another brick, another stone, built into the temple of his life will he develop the insight which will enable him to recognise his own unstable handiwork, the unflinching manliness to acknowledge it, and the courage to build more nobly and enduringly.

Painful burdens are necessary, but only so long as we lack love and wisdom.

The Temple of Blessedness lies beyond the outer courts of suffering and humiliation and to reach it the pilgrim must pass through the outer courts. For a time he will linger in the outer, but only so long as, through his own imperfect understanding, he mistakes it for the inner. While he pities himself and confounds suffering with holiness he will remain in suffering: but when, casting off the last unholy rag of self-pity, he perceives that suffering is a means and not an end, that it is a state self-originated and self-propagated, then, converted and right-minded, he will rapidly pass through the outer courts, and reach the inner abode of peace.

Suffering does not originate in the perfect but in the imperfect; it does not mark the complete but the incomplete; it can, therefore, be transcended. Its self-born cause can be found, investigated, comprehended, and forever removed.

It is true therefore, that we must pass through agony to rest, through loneliness to peace; but let the sufferer not forget that it is a "passing through;" that the agony is a gateway and not a habitation; that the loneliness is a pathway and not a destination; and that a little farther on he will come to the painless and blissful repose.

Little by little is a burden accumulated; imperceptibly and by degrees is its weight increased. A thoughtless impulse, a gross self-indulgence, a blind passion yielded to and gratified again and again; an impure thought fostered, a cruel word uttered, a foolish thing done time after time, and at last the gathered weight of many follies becomes oppressive. At first, and for a time, the weight is not felt; but it is being added to day after day, and the time comes when the accumulated burden is felt in all its galling weight, when the bitter fruits of selfishness are gathered, and the heart is troubled with the weariness of life. When this period arrives let the sufferer look to himself; let him search for the blessed way of burden-dropping, finding which he will find wisdom to live better, purity to live sweeter, love to live nobler; will find, in the reversal of that conduct by which his burdens were accumulated, light-hearted nights and days, cheerful action, and unclouded joy.

> "Come out of the world—come above it -
> Up over its crosses and graves;
> Though the green earth is fair and I love it,
> We must love it as masters, not slaves,
> Come up where the dust never rises -
> But only the perfume of flowers -
> And your life shall be glad with surprises
> Of beautiful hours."

24

THE REALIZATION OF SELFLESS LOVE

It is said that Michael Angelo saw in every rough block of stone a thing of beauty awaiting the master-hand to bring it into reality. Even so, within each there reposes the Divine Image awaiting the master-hand of Faith and the chisel of Patience to bring it into manifestation. And that Divine Image is revealed and realized as stainless, selfless Love.

Hidden deep in every human heart, though frequently covered up with a mass of hard and almost impenetrable accretions, is the spirit of Divine Love, whose holy and spotless essence is undying and eternal. It is the Truth in man; it is that which belongs to the Supreme: that which is real and immortal. All else changes and passes away; this alone is permanent and imperishable; and to realize this Love by ceaseless diligence in the practice of the highest righteousness, to live in it and to become fully conscious in it, is to enter into immortality here and now, is to become one with Truth, one with God, one with the central Heart of all things, and to know our own divine and eternal nature.

To reach this Love, to understand and experience it, one must work with great persistency and diligence upon his heart and mind, must ever renew his patience and keep strong his faith, for there will be much to remove, much to accomplish before the Divine Image is revealed in all its glorious beauty.

He who strives to reach and to accomplish the divine will be tried to the very uttermost; and this is absolutely necessary, for how else could one acquire that sublime patience without which there is no real wisdom, no divinity? Ever and anon, as he proceeds, all his work will seem to be futile, and his efforts appear to be thrown away. Now and then a hasty touch will mar his image, and perhaps when he imagines his work is almost completed he will find what he imagined to be the beautiful form of Divine Love utterly destroyed, and he must begin again with his past bitter experience to guide and help him. But he who has resolutely set himself to realize the Highest recognizes no such thing as defeat. All failures are apparent, not real. Every slip, every fall, every return to selfishness is a lesson learned, an experience gained, from which a golden grain of wisdom is extracted, helping the striver toward the accomplishment of his lofty object. To recognize

"That of our vices we can frame
A ladder if we will but tread
Beneath our feet each deed of shame,"

is to enter the way that leads unmistakably toward the Divine, and the failings of one who Thus, recognizes are so many dead selves, upon which he rises, as upon stepping-stones, to higher things.

Once come to regard your failings, your sorrows and sufferings as so many voices telling you plainly where you are weak and faulty, where you fall below the true and the divine, you will then begin to ceaselessly watch yourself, and every slip, every pang of pain will show you where you are to set to work, and what you have to remove out of your heart in order to bring it nearer to the likeness of the Divine, nearer to the Perfect Love. And as you proceed, day by day detaching yourself more and more from the inward selfishness the Love that is selfless will gradually become revealed to you. And when you are growing patient and calm, when your petulances, tempers, and irritabilities are passing away from you, and the more powerful lusts and prejudices cease to dominate and enslave you, then you will know that the divine is awakening within you, that you are drawing near to the eternal Heart, that you are not far from that selfless Love, the possession of which is peace and immortality.

Divine Love is distinguished from human loves in this supremely important particular, *it is free from partiality*. Human loves cling to a particular object to the exclusion of all else, and when that object is removed, great and deep is the resultant suffering to the one who loves. Divine Love embraces the whole universe, and, without clinging to any part, yet contains within itself the whole, and he who comes to it by gradually purifying and broadening his human loves until all the selfish and impure elements are burnt out of them, ceases from suffering. It is because human loves are narrow and confined and mingled with selfishness that they cause suffering. No suffering can result from that Love which is so absolutely pure that it seeks nothing for itself. Nevertheless, human loves are absolutely necessary as steps toward the Divine, and no soul is prepared to partake of Divine Love until it has become capable of the deepest and most intense human love. It is only by passing through human loves and human sufferings that Divine Love is reached and realized.

All human loves are perishable like the forms to which they cling; but there is a Love that is imperishable, and that does not cling to appearances.

All human loves are counterbalanced by human hates; but there is a Love that admits of no opposite or reaction; divine and free from all taint of self, that sheds its fragrance on all alike.

Human loves are reflections of the Divine Love, and draw the soul nearer to the reality, the Love that knows neither sorrow nor change.

It is well that the mother, clinging with passionate tenderness to the little helpless form of flesh that lies on her bosom, should be overwhelmed with the dark waters of sorrow when she sees it laid in the cold earth. It is well that her tears should flow and her heart ache, for only Thus, can she be reminded of the evanescent nature of the joys and objects of sense, and be drawn nearer to the eternal and imperishable Reality.

It is well that lover, brother, sister, husband, wife should suffer deep anguish, and be enveloped in gloom when the visible object of their affections is torn from them, so that they may learn to turn their affections toward the invisible Source of all, where alone abiding satisfaction is to be found.

It is well that the proud, the ambitious, the self-seeking, should suffer defeat, humiliation, and misfortune; that they should pass through the scorching fires of affliction; for only Thus, can the wayward soul be brought to reflect upon the enigma of life; only Thus, can the heart be softened and purified, and prepared to receive the Truth.

When the sting of anguish penetrates the heart of human love; when gloom and loneliness and desertion cloud the soul of friendship and trust, then it is that the heart turns toward the sheltering love of the Eternal, and finds rest in its silent peace. And whosoever comes to this Love is not turned away comfortless, is not pierced with anguish nor surrounded with gloom; and is never deserted in the dark hour of trial.

The glory of Divine Love can only be revealed in the heart that is chastened by sorrow, and the image of the heavenly state can only be perceived and realized when the lifeless, formless accretions of ignorance and self are hewn away.

Only that Love that seeks no personal gratification or reward, that does not make distinctions, and that leaves behind no heartaches, can be called divine.

Men, clinging to self and to the comfortless shadows of evil, are in the habit of thinking of divine Love as something belonging to a God who is out of reach; as something outside themselves, and that must forever remain outside. Truly, the Love of God is ever beyond the reach of self, but when the heart and mind are emptied of self then the selfless Love, the supreme Love, the Love that is of God or Good becomes an inward and abiding reality.

And this inward realization of holy Love is none other than the Love of Christ that is so much talked about and so little comprehended. The Love that not only saves the soul from sin, but lifts it also above the power of temptation.

But how may one attain to this sublime realization? The answer which Truth has always given, and will ever give to this question is,--"Empty thyself, and I will fill thee." Divine Love cannot be known until self is dead, for self is the denial of Love, and how can that which is known be also denied? Not until the stone of self is rolled away from the sepulcher of the soul does the immortal Christ, the pure Spirit of Love, hitherto crucified, dead and buried, cast off the bands of ignorance, and come forth in all the majesty of His resurrection.

You believe that the Christ of Nazareth was put to death and rose again. I do not say you err in that belief; but if you refuse to believe that the gentle spirit of Love is crucified daily upon the dark cross of your selfish desires, then, I say, you err in this unbelief, and have not yet perceived, even afar off, the Love of Christ.

You say that you have tasted of salvation in the Love of Christ. Are you saved from your temper, your irritability, your vanity, your personal dislikes, your judgment and condemnation of others? If not, from what are you saved, and wherein have you realized the transforming Love of Christ?

He who has realized the Love that is divine has become a new man, and has ceased to be swayed and dominated by the old elements of self. He is known for his patience, his purity, his self-control, his deep charity of heart, and his unalterable sweetness.

Divine or selfless Love is not a mere sentiment or emotion; it is a state of knowledge which destroys the dominion of evil and the belief in evil, and lifts the soul into the joyful realization of the supreme Good. To the divinely wise, knowledge and Love are one and inseparable.

It is toward the complete realization of this divine Love that the whole world is moving; it was for this purpose that the universe came into existence, and every grasping at happiness, every reaching out of the soul toward objects, ideas and ideals, is an effort to realize it. But the world does not realize this Love at present because it is grasping at the fleeting shadow and ignoring, in its blindness, the substance. And so suffering and sorrow continue, and must continue until the world, taught by its self-inflicted pains, discovers the Love that is selfless, the wisdom that is calm and full of peace.

And this Love, this Wisdom, this Peace, this tranquil state of mind and heart may be attained to, may be realized by all who are willing and ready to yield up self, and who are prepared to humbly enter into a comprehension of all that the giving up of self involves. There is no arbitrary power in the universe, and the strongest chains of fate by which men are bound are self-forged. Men are chained to that which causes suffering because they desire to be so, because they love their chains, because they think their little dark prison of self is sweet and beautiful, and they are afraid that if they desert that prison they will lose all that is real and worth having.

"Ye suffer from yourselves, none else compels,
None other holds ye that ye live and die."

And the indwelling power which forged the chains and built around itself the dark and narrow prison, can break away when it desires and wills to do so, and the soul does will to do so when it has discovered the worthlessness of its prison, when long suffering has prepared it for the reception of the boundless Light and Love.

As the shadow follows the form, and as smoke comes after fire, so effect follows cause, and suffering and bliss follow the thoughts and deeds of men. There is no effect in the world around us but has its hidden or revealed cause, and that cause is in accordance with absolute justice. Men reap a harvest of suffering because in the near or distant past they have sown the seeds of evil; they reap a harvest of bliss also as a result of their own sowing of the seeds of good. Let a man meditate upon this, let him strive to understand it, and he will then begin to sow only seeds of good, and will burn up the tares and weeds which he has formerly grown in the garden of his heart.

The world does not understand the Love that is selfless because it is engrossed in the pursuit of its own pleasures, and cramped within the narrow limits of perishable interests mistaking, in its ignorance, those pleasures and interests for real and abiding things. Caught in the flames of fleshly lusts, and burning with anguish, it sees not the pure and peaceful beauty of Truth. Feeding upon the swinish husks of error and self-delusion, it is shut out from the mansion of all-seeing Love.

Not having this Love, not understanding it, men institute innumerable reforms which involve no inward sacrifice, and each imagines that his reform is going to right the world forever, while he himself continues to propagate evil by engaging it in his own heart. That only can be called reform which tends to reform the human heart, for all evil has its rise there, and not until the world, ceasing from selfishness and party strife, has learned the lesson of divine Love, will it realize the Golden Age of universal blessedness.

Let the rich cease to despise the poor, and the poor to condemn the rich; let the greedy learn how to give, and the lustful how to grow pure; let the partisan cease from strife, and the uncharitable begin to forgive; let the envious endeavor to rejoice with others, and the slanderers grow ashamed of their conduct. Let men and women take this course, and, lo! the Golden Age is at hand. He, therefore, who purifies his own heart is the world's greatest benefactor.

Yet, though the world is, and will be for many ages to come, shut out from that Age of Gold, which is the realization of selfless Love, you, if you are willing, may enter it now, by rising above your selfish self; if you will pass from prejudice, hatred, and condemnation, to gentle and forgiving love.

Where hatred, dislike, and condemnation are, selfless Love does not abide. It resides only in the heart that has ceased from all condemnation.

You say, "How can I love the drunkard, the hypocrite, the sneak, the murderer? I am compelled to dislike and condemn such men." It is true you cannot love such men *emotionally*, but when you say that you must perforce dislike and condemn them you show that you are not acquainted with the Great over-ruling Love; for it is possible to attain to such a state of interior enlightenment as will enable you to perceive the train of causes by which these men have become as they are, to enter into their intense sufferings, and to know the certainty of their ultimate purification. Possessed of such knowledge it will be utterly impossible for you any longer to dislike or condemn them, and you will always think of them with perfect calmness and deep compassion.

If you love people and speak of them with praise until they in some way thwart you, or do something of which you disapprove, and then you dislike them and speak of them with dispraise, you are not governed by the Love which is of God. If, in your heart, you are continually arraigning and condemning others, selfless Love is hidden from you.

He who knows that Love is at the heart of all things, and has realized the all-sufficing power of that Love, has no room in his heart for condemnation.

Men, not knowing this Love, constitute themselves judge and executioner of their fellows, forgetting that there is the Eternal Judge and Executioner, and in so far as men deviate from them in their own views, their particular reforms and methods, they brand them as fanatical, unbalanced, lacking judgment, sincerity, and honesty; in so far as others approximate to their own standard do they look upon them as being everything that is admirable. Such are the men who are centered in self. But he whose heart is centered in the supreme Love does not so brand and classify men; does not seek to convert men to his own views, not to convince them of the superiority of his methods. Knowing the Law of Love, he lives it, and maintains the same calm attitude of mind and sweetness of heart toward all. The debased and the virtuous, the foolish and the wise, the learned and the unlearned, the selfish and the unselfish receive alike the benediction of his tranquil thought.

You can only attain to this supreme knowledge, this divine Love by unremitting endeavor in self-discipline, and by gaining victory after victory over yourself. Only the pure in heart see God, and when your heart is sufficiently purified you will enter into the New Birth, and the Love that does not die, nor change, nor end in pain and sorrow will be awakened within you, and you will be at peace.

He who strives for the attainment of divine Love is ever seeking to overcome the spirit of condemnation, for where there is pure spiritual knowledge, condemnation cannot exist, and only in the heart that has become incapable of condemnation is Love perfected and fully realized.

The Christian condemns the Atheist; the Atheist satirizes the Christian; the Catholic and Protestant are ceaselessly engaged in wordy warfare, and the spirit of strife and hatred rules where peace and love should be.

"He that hateth his brother is a murderer," a crucifier of the divine Spirit of Love; and until you can regard men of all religions and of no religion with the same impartial spirit, with all freedom from dislike, and with perfect equanimity, you have yet to strive for that Love which bestows upon its possessor freedom and salvation.

The realization of divine knowledge, selfless Love, utterly destroys the spirit of condemnation, disperses all evil, and lifts the consciousness to that height of pure vision where Love, Goodness, Justice are seen to be universal, supreme, all-conquering, indestructible.

Train your mind in strong, impartial, and gentle thought; train your heart in purity and compassion; train your tongue to silence and to true and stainless speech; so shall you enter the way of holiness and peace, and shall ultimately realize the immortal Love. So living, without seeking to convert, you will convince; without arguing, you will teach; not cherishing ambition, the wise will find you out; and without striving to gain men's opinions, you will subdue their hearts. For Love is all-conquering, all-powerful; and the thoughts, and deeds, and words of Love can never perish.

To know that Love is universal, supreme, all-sufficing; to be freed from the trammels of evil; to be quit of the inward unrest; to know that all men are striving to realize the Truth each in his own way; to be satisfied, sorrowless, serene; this is peace; this is gladness; this is immortality; this is Divinity; this is the realization of selfless Love.

I stood upon the shore, and saw the rocks
Resist the onslaught of the mighty sea,
And when I thought how all the countless shocks
They had withstood through an eternity,
I said, "To wear away this solid main
The ceaseless efforts of the waves are vain."

But when I thought how they the rocks had rent,
And saw the sand and shingles at my feet
(Poor passive remnants of resistance spent)
Tumbled and tossed where they the waters meet,
Then saw I ancient landmarks 'neath the waves,
And knew the waters held the stones their slaves.

I saw the mighty work the waters wrought
By patient softness and unceasing flow;
How they the proudest promontory brought
Unto their feet, and massy hills laid low;
How the soft drops the adamantine wall
Conquered at last, and brought it to its fall.

And then I knew that hard, resisting sin
Should yield at last to Love's soft ceaseless roll
Coming and going, ever flowing in
Upon the proud rocks of the human soul;
That all resistance should be spent and past,
And every heart yield unto it at last.

25

LIGHT ON LIFE'S SORROWS

There is great sorrow in the world. This is one of the supreme facts of life. Grief and affliction visit every heart, and many that are today reveling in hilarious joy or sinful riot, will tomorrow be smitten low with sorrow. Suddenly, and with swift and silent certainty, comes its poignant arrow, entering the human heart, slaying its joy, laying low its hopes, and shattering all its earthly plans and prospects. Then the humbled, smitten soul reflects, and enters deeply and sympathetically into the hidden meanings of human life.

In the dark times of sorrow, men and women approach very near to Truth. When in one brief hour the built up hopes of many years of toil fall like a toy palace, and all earthly pleasures burst and vanish like petty bubbles in the grasp, then the crushed spirit, bewildered, tempest-tossed, and without a refuge, gropes in dumb anguish for the Eternal, and seeks its abiding peace.

"Blessed are they that mourn," said the Teacher of the West, and the Teacher of the East declared that, "Where there is great suffering there is great bliss." Both of these sayings express the truth that sorrow is a teacher and purifier. Sorrow is not the end of life—though it is, in its consummation, the end of the worldly life—it leads the bewildered spirit into rest and safety; for the end of sorrow is joy and peace.

Strong searcher for Truth! Strenuous fighter against self and passion! Seasons of sorrow must be your portion for a time. While any vestige of self remains, temptations will assail you; the veil of illusion will cloud your spiritual vision, producing sorrow and unrest. When heavy clouds settle down upon your spirit, accept the darkness as your own, and pass through it bravely into the cloudless light beyond. Bear well in mind that nothing can overtake you that does not belong to you and that is not for your eternal good. As the poet has truly sung—

> Nor space nor time, nor deep nor high Can keep my own away from me.

And not alone are the bright things of life yours; the dark things are yours also.

When one has reached the lowest point of sorrow; when, weak and exhausted, and overcome with a sense of powerlessness, he cries to God for help, and there comes no answering comfort and no relief—then, discovering the painfulness of sorrow and the insufficiency of prayer alone, he is ready to enter the path of self-renunciation, ready to purify his heart, ready to practice self-control, ready to become a spiritual athlete, and to develop that divine and invincible strength which is born of self-mastery.

He will find the cause of sorrow in his own heart, and will remove it. He will learn to stand alone; not craving sympathy from any, but giving it to all. Not thoughtlessly sinning and remorsefully repenting, but studying how not to commit sin. Humbled by innumerable defeats, and chastened by many sufferings, he will learn how to act blamelessly toward others, how to be gentle and strong, kind and steadfast, compassionate and wise.

Thus, he will gradually rise above sorrow, and at last Truth will dawn upon his mind, and he will understand the meaning of abiding peace. His mental eye will be open to perceive the Cosmic Order. He will be blessed with the Vision of the Law, and will receive the Beatific Bliss.

When the true order of things is perceived, sorrow is transcended. When the contracted personal self, which hugs its own fleeting pleasures and broods over its own petty disappointments and dissatisfactions, is broken up and cast away, then the larger life of Truth enters the mind, bringing bliss and peace; and the Universal Will takes the place of self. The individual becomes one with humanity. He forgets self in his love for all. His sorrow is swallowed up in the bliss of Truth.

Thus, when you have, by experience, entered completely into the sorrow that is never lifted from the heart of humankind; when you have reaped and eaten all the bitter fruits of your own wrong thoughts and deeds—then divine compassion for all suffering beings will be born in your heart, healing all your wounds and drying all your tears. You will rise again into a new and heavenly life, where the sting of sorrow cannot enter, for there is no self there. After the crucifixion comes the transfiguration; the sorrowless state is reached through sorrow, and "the wise do not grieve."

Ever remember this—in the midst of sin and sorrow there abides the world of Truth. Redemption is at hand. The troubled may find peace; the impure may find purity. Healing awaits the broken-hearted. The weak will be adorned with strength, and the downtrodden will be lifted up and glorified.

26

THE WAY OUT OF UNDESIRABLE CONDITIONS

Having seen and realized that evil is but a passing shadow thrown, by the intercepting self, across the transcendent Form of the Eternal Good, and that the world is a mirror in which each sees a reflection of himself, we now ascend, by firm and easy steps, to that plane of perception whereon is seen and realized the Vision of the Law.

With this realization comes the knowledge that everything is included in a ceaseless interaction of cause and effect, and that nothing can possibly be divorced from law.

From the most trivial thought, word, or act of man, up to the groupings of the celestial bodies, law reigns supreme. No arbitrary condition can, even for one moment, exist, for such a condition would be a denial and an annihilation of law.

Every condition of life is, therefore, bound up in an orderly and harmonious sequence, and the secret and cause of every condition is contained within itself, The law, "Whatsoever a man sows that shall he also reap," is inscribed in flaming letters upon the portal of Eternity, and none can deny it, none can cheat it, none can escape it.

He who puts his hand in the fire must suffer the burning until such time as it has worked itself out, and neither curses nor prayers can avail to alter it.

And precisely the same law governs the realm of mind. Hatred, anger, jealousy, envy, lust, covetousness, all these are fires which bum, and whoever even so much as touches them must suffer the torments of burning.

All these conditions of mind are rightly called "evil," for they are the efforts of the soul to subvert, in its ignorance, the law, an they, therefore, lead to chaos and confusion within, and are sooner or later actualized in the outward circumstances as disease, failure, and misfortune, coupled with grief, pain, and despair.

Whereas love, gentleness, good-will, purity, are cooling airs which breathe peace upon the soul that woes them, and, being in harmony with the Eternal Law, they become actualized in the form of health, peaceful surroundings, and undeviating success and good fortune.

A thorough understanding of this Great Law which permeates the universe leads to the acquirement of that state of mind known as obedience.

To know that justice, harmony, and love are supreme in the universe is likewise to know that all adverse and painful conditions are the result of our own disobedience to that Law.

Such knowledge leads to strength and power, and it is upon such knowledge alone that a true life and an enduring success and happiness can be built.

To be patient under all circumstances, and to accept all conditions as necessary factors in your training, is to rise superior to all painful conditions, and to overcome them with an overcoming which is sure, and which leaves no fear of their return, for by the power of obedience to law they are utterly slain.

Such an obedient one is working in harmony with the law, has in fact, identified himself with the law, and whatsoever he conquers he conquers forever, whatsoever he builds can never be destroyed.

The cause of all power, as of all weakness, is within; the secret of all happiness as of all misery is likewise within.

There is no progress apart from unfoldment within, and no sure foothold of prosperity or peace except by orderly advancement in knowledge.

You say you are chained by circumstances; you cry out for better opportunities, for a wider scope, for improved physical conditions, and perhaps you inwardly curse the fate that binds you hand and foot.

It is for you that I write; it is to you that I speak. Listen, and let my words burn themselves into your heart, for that which I say to you is truth:

You may bring about that improved condition in your outward life which you desire, if you will unswervingly resolve to improve your inner life.

I know this pathway looks barren at its commencement (truth always does, it is only error and delusion which are at first inviting and fascinating,) but if you undertake to walk it; if you perseveringly discipline your mind, eradicating your weaknesses, and allowing your soul-forces and spiritual powers to unfold themselves, you will be astonished at the magical changes which will be brought about in your outward life.

As you proceed, golden opportunities will be strewn across your path, and the power and judgment to properly utilize them will spring up within you. Genial friends will come unbidden to you; sympathetic souls will be drawn to you as the needle is to the magnet; and books and all outward aids that you require will come to you unsought.

Perhaps the chains of poverty hang heavily upon you, and

you are friendless and alone, and you long with an intense longing that your load may be lightened; but the load continues, and you seem to be enveloped in an ever-increasing darkness.

Perhaps you complain, you bewail your lot; you blame your birth, your parents, your employer, or the unjust Powers who have bestowed upon you so undeservedly poverty and hardship, and upon another affluence and ease.

Cease your complaining and fretting; none of these things which you blame are the cause of your poverty; the cause is within yourself, and where the cause is, there is the remedy.

The very fact that you are a complainer, shows that you deserve your lot; shows that you lack that faith which is the ground of all effort and progress.

There is no room for a complainer in a universe of law, and worry is soul-suicide. By your very attitude of mind you are strengthening the chains which bind you, and are drawing about you the darkness by which you are enveloped, Alter your outlook upon life, and your outward life will alter.

Build yourself up in the faith and knowledge, and make yourself worthy of better surroundings and wider opportunities. Be sure, first of all, that you are making the best of what you have.

Do not delude yourself into supposing that you can step into greater advantages whilst overlooking smaller ones, for if you could, the advantage would be impermanent and you would quickly fall back again in order to learn the lesson which you had neglected.

As the child at school must master one standard before passing onto the next, so, before you can have that greater good which you so desire, must you faithfully employ that which you already possess.

The parable of the talents is a beautiful story illustrative of this truth, for does it not plainly show that if we misuse, neglect, or degrade that which we possess, be it ever so mean and insignificant, even that little will be taken from us, for, by our conduct we show that we are unworthy of it.

Perhaps you are living in a small cottage, and are surrounded by unhealthy and vicious influences.

You desire a larger and more sanitary residence. Then you must fit yourself for such a residence by first of all making your cottage as far as possible a little paradise. Keep it spotlessly clean. Make it look as pretty and sweet as your limited means will allow. Cook your plain food with all care, and arrange your humble table as tastefully as you possibly can.

If you cannot afford a carpet, let your rooms be carpeted with smiles and welcomes, fastened down with the nails of kind words driven in with the hammer of patience. Such a carpet will not fade in the sun, and constant use will never wear it away.

By so ennobling your present surroundings you will rise above them, and above the need of them, and at the right time you will pass on into the better house and surroundings which have all along been waiting for you, and which you have fitted yourself to occupy.

Perhaps you desire more time for thought and effort, and feel that your hours of labor are too hard and long. Then see to it that you are utilizing to the fullest possible extent what little spare time you have.

It is useless to desire more time, if you are already wasting what little you have; for you would only grow more indolent and indifferent.

Even poverty and lack of time and leisure are not the evils that you imagine they are, and if they hinder you in your progress, it is because you have clothed them in your own weaknesses, and the evil that you see in them is really in yourself. Endeavor to fully and completely realize that in so far as you shape and mould your mind, you are the maker of your destiny, and as, by the transmuting power of self-discipline you realize this more and more, you will come to see that these so-called evils may be converted into blessings.

You will then utilize your poverty for the cultivation of patience, hope and courage; and your lack of time in the gaining of promptness of action and decision of mind, by seizing the precious moments as they present themselves for your acceptance.

As in the rankest soil the most beautiful flowers are grown, so in the dark soil of poverty the choicest flowers of humanity have developed and bloomed.

Where there are difficulties to cope with, and unsatisfactory conditions to overcome, there virtue most flourishes and manifests its glory.

It may be that you are in the employ of a tyrannous master or mistress, and you feel that you are harshly treated. Look upon this also as necessary to your training. Return your employer's unkindness with gentleness and forgiveness.

Practice unceasingly patience and self-control. Turn the disadvantage to account by utilizing it for the gaining of mental and spiritual strength, and by your silent example and influence you will Thus, be teaching your employer, will be helping him to grow ashamed of his conduct, and will, at the same time, be lifting yourself up to that height of spiritual attainment by which you will be enabled to step into new and more congenial surroundings at the time when they are presented to you.

27

THE TWO MASTERS, SELF AND TRUTH

Upon the battlefield of the human soul two masters are ever contending for the crown of supremacy, for the kingship and dominion of the heart; the master of self, called also the "Prince of this world," and the master of Truth, called also the Father God. The master self is that rebellious one whose weapons are passion, pride, avarice, vanity, self-will, implements of darkness; the master Truth is that meek and lowly one whose weapons are gentleness, patience, purity, sacrifice, humility, love, instruments of Light.

In every soul the battle is waged, and as a soldier cannot engage at once in two opposing armies, so every heart is enlisted either in the ranks of self or of Truth. There is no half-and-half course; "There is self and there is Truth; where self is, Truth is not, where Truth is, self is not." Thus, spake Buddha, the teacher of Truth, and Jesus, the manifested Christ, declared that "No man can serve two masters; for either he will hate the one and love the other; or else he will hold to the one, and despise the other. Ye cannot serve God and Mammon."

Truth is so simple, so absolutely undeviating and uncompromising that it admits of no complexity, no turning, no qualification. Self is ingenious, crooked, and, governed by subtle and snaky desire, admits of endless turnings and qualifications, and the deluded worshipers of self vainly imagine that they can gratify every worldly desire, and at the same time possess the Truth. But the lovers of Truth worship Truth with the sacrifice of self, and ceaselessly guard themselves against worldliness and self-seeking.

Self is the denial of Truth. Truth is the denial of self. As you let self die, you will be reborn in Truth. As you cling to self, Truth will be hidden from you.

Whilst you cling to self, your path will be beset with difficulties, and repeated pains, sorrows, and disappointments will be your lot. There are no difficulties in Truth, and coming to Truth, you will be freed from all sorrow and disappointment.

The signs by which the Truth-lover is known are unmistakable. Hear the Holy Krishna declare them, in Sir Edwin Arnold's beautiful rendering of the "Bhagavad Gita":

"Fearlessness, singleness of soul, the will
Always to strive for wisdom; opened hand
And governed appetites; and piety,
And love of lonely study; humbleness,
Uprightness, heed to injure nought which lives
Truthfulness, slowness unto wrath, a mind
That lightly letteth go what others prize;
And equanimity, and charity
Which spieth no man's faults; and tenderness
Towards all that suffer; a contented heart,
Fluttered by no desires; a bearing mild,
Modest and grave, with manhood nobly mixed,
With patience, fortitude and purity;
An unrevengeful spirit, never given

To rate itself too high--such be the signs,
O Indian Prince! of him whose feet are set
On that fair path which leads to heavenly birth!"

28

THE REALIZATION OF PROSPERITY

It is granted only to the heart that abounds with integrity, trust, generosity and love to realize true prosperity. The heart that is not possessed of these qualities cannot know prosperity, for prosperity, like happiness, is not an outward possession, but an inward realization.

The greedy man may become a millionaire, but he will always be wretched, and mean, and poor, and will even consider himself outwardly poor so long as there is a man in the world who is richer than himself, whilst the upright, the open-handed and loving will realize a full and rich prosperity, even though their outward possessions may be small.

He is poor who is dissatisfied; he is rich who is contented with what he has, and he is richer who is generous with what he has.

When we contemplate the fact that the universe is abounding in all good things, material as well as spiritual, and compare it with man's blind eagerness to secure a few gold coins, or a few acres of dirt, it is then that we realize how dark and ignorant selfishness is; it is then that we know that self-seeking is self-destruction.

Nature gives all, without reservation, and loses nothing; man, grasping all, loses everything.

If you would realize true prosperity do not settle down, as many have done, into the belief that if you do right everything will go wrong. Do not allow the word "competition" to shake your faith in the supremacy of righteousness.

I care not what men may say about the "laws of competition," for do I not know the unchangeable Law, which shall one day put them all to rout, and which puts them to rout even now in the heart and life of the righteous man?

And knowing this Law I can contemplate all dishonesty with undisturbed repose, for I know where certain destruction awaits it. Under all circumstances do that which you believe to be right, and trust the Law; trust the Divine Power that is imminent in the universe, and it will never desert you, and you will always be protected.

By such a trust all your losses will be converted into gains, and all curses which threaten will be transmuted into blessings. Never let go of integrity, generosity, and love, for these, coupled with energy, will lift you into the truly prosperous state.

Do not believe the world when it tells you that you must always attend to "number one" first, and to others afterwards. To do this is not to think of others at all, but only of one's own comforts.

To those who practice this the day will come when they will be deserted by all, and when they cry out in their loneliness and anguish there will be no one to hear and help them. To consider one's self before all others is to cramp and warp and hinder every noble and divine impulse.

Let your soul expand, let your heart reach out to others in loving and generous warmth, and great and lasting will be your joy, and all prosperity will come to you. Those who have wandered from the highway of righteousness guard themselves against competition; those who always pursue the right need not to trouble about such defense.

29

HAPPY ENDINGS

"Such is the Law which moves to righteousness,
Which none at last can turn aside or stay;
The heart of it is Love, the end of it
Is peace and consummation sweet. Obey."

—The Light of Asia

"So, haply, when thy task shall end,
The wrong shall lose itself in right,
And all thy week-day Sabbaths blend
With the long Sabbath of the Light!"

—Whittier

Life has many happy endings, because it has much that is noble and pure and beautiful. Although there is much sin and ignorance in the world, many tears, and much pain and sorrow, there is also much purity and knowledge, many smiles, and much healing and gladness. No pure thought, no unselfish deed can fall short of its felicitous result, and every such result is a happy consummation.

A pleasant home is a happy ending; a successful life is a happy ending; a task well and faithfully done is a happy ending; to be surrounded by kind friends is a happy ending. A quarrel put away, grudges wiped out, unkind words confessed and forgiven, friend restored to friend—all these are happy endings. To find that which one has long and tediously sought; to be restored from tears to gladness; to awaken in the bright sunlight out of the painful nightmare of sin, to strike, after much searching, the Heavenly Way in life—these are, indeed, blessed consummations.

He who looks for, finds, and enters the byways which I have indicated will come to this one without seeking it, for his whole life will be filled with happy endings. He who begins right and continues right does not need to desire and search for felicitous results; they are already at hand; they follow as consequences; they are the certainties, the realities of life.

There are happy endings which belong solely to the material world; these are transient, and they pass away. These are happy endings which belong to the spiritual world; these are eternal, and they do not pass away. Sweet are companionships, pleasures, and material comforts, but they change and fade away. Sweeter still are Purity, Wisdom, and the knowledge of Truth, and these never change nor fade away. Wherever a man goes in this world he can take his worldly possessions with him; but soon he must part company with them, and if he stands upon these alone, deriving all his happiness from them, he will come to a spiritual ending of great emptiness and want. But he has attained to the possession of spiritual things can never be deprived of his source of happiness: he will never have to part company with it, and wherever he goes in the whole universe he will carry his possession with him. His spiritual end will be the fulness of joy.

away, grudges wiped out, soiled ways corrected and forgiven, friend restored to friend—all these are [illegible] endings. To find that which one has long and unselfishly sought, to be rejoiced from tears to gladness, to awaken to the light that puts out the purpled nightmare of sin, as the [illegible] singing the Heavenly Way in life—all these are happy consummations.

In some works [illegible] and sorrows are [illegible] which have [illegible] with [illegible] for his whole day will be filled with [illegible]. He who [illegible] right and considers right [illegible] need not [illegible] for [illegible] results, they are already [illegible], [illegible] consequences [illegible] the [illegible] and [illegible] of life.

[illegible] happy endings which belong [illegible] in the natural world: these are transient, and they pass away. [illegible] happy endings which belong to the spiritual world: they are eternal and they do not pass away. Wealth, comfort, pleasures, [illegible] and material enjoyments, these change and fade away. But [illegible] still untiring Wisdom and the knowledge of Truth, these never change nor fade away. Whatever a man does in this world he can take his worldly possessions with him [illegible] part company with them, and if he stands upon these alone, deriving all his happiness from them, he will come to a spiritual ending of great sorrowfulness and woe. But he who has attained to the possession of spiritual things can never be deprived of these sources of happiness; he will never have to part company with it, and wherever he goes in the whole universe he will carry his possession with him. His spiritual end will be the fulness of joy.